𝒯his book's journey began with

....

and the knowledge within is now being
passed on to and shared with

....

....

....

....

....

THE DAY MY VAGINA BROKE

What they *don't* tell you about childbirth

STEPHANIE THOMPSON

About the author

First and foremost, Stephanie Thompson is an awesome and brave mumma (and wife). Her long journey to becoming a mum is her greatest achievement. Her 'never-die' attitude and resilience to adversity was just not going to let cancer or birth trauma stop her from trying to be the 'best' mum she can be.

With over 15 years' experience working as an educator and leader, she knows how important advocacy is for making real change. After completing her degree in education, she worked as a critical responder in Child Protection for a few years before heading into the classrooms of public schools across Sydney for the next decade.

Prior to the birth of her babies, she was an education consultant for some of the top private schools across the eastern states of Australia, while also running a small tea business and competing in triathlons. Busy is what she does best.

Stephanie lives with her loving husband, two little people and two fat cats on the south coast of New South Wales. She isn't able to be a teacher, a triathlete or tea business owner anymore. The trauma from giving birth has left her body broken.

But, of course, that is not the end of the story. After looking in all the wrong places for her resolve, she discovered writing. Writing is now how she is helping to make way for change in this childbirth space.

Stephanie created the 'Bravemumma' community and is working hard to advocate for the sisterhood to band together and support one another in what is already a difficult time. Her main aim is to ensure women can feel empowered to make informed decisions about their birth choices – and beyond into motherhood.

When she manages to find a spare 32 minutes, she enjoys watching *The Letdown*, while folding the Mt Washmore of baby clothes with a cup of tea.

First published in 2019 by Stephanie Thompson

© Stephanie Thompson 2019
The moral rights of the author have been asserted

All rights reserved. Except as permitted under the *Australian Copyright Act 1968* (for example, a fair dealing for the purposes of study, research, criticism or review), no part of this book may be reproduced, stored in a retrieval system, communicated or transmitted in any form or by any means without prior written permission.

All inquiries should be made to the author.

A catalogue entry for this book is available from the National Library of Australia.

ISBN: 978-1-925921-34-2

Project management and text design by Michael Hanrahan Publishing
Cover design by Kerry Milin, Production Works Australia

The material in this publication is of the nature of general comment only, and does not represent professional advice. It is not intended to provide specific guidance for particular circumstances and it should not be relied on as the basis for any decision to take action or not take action on any matter which it covers. Readers should obtain professional advice where appropriate, before making any such decision. To the maximum extent permitted by law, the author and publisher disclaim all responsibility and liability to any person, arising directly or indirectly from any person taking or not taking action based on the information in this publication.

Contents

Introduction **1**

Chapter 1: How did we get here? **11**

Chapter 2: Pre-birth – a bun in the oven **19**

Chapter 3: The birth – baking day **31**

Chapter 4: After birth **43**

Chapter 5: After the after birth **57**

Chapter 6: The (un)happy little family **61**

Chapter 7: The costs **77**

Chapter 8: Never trust a lawyer, they say ... legals and insurance **97**

Chapter 9: My workarounds **111**

Chapter 10: Mumma's back – to break the cycle of judgement and silence **121**

Chapter 11: Advocacy **127**

Where to from here? **135**

FAQs **139**

A note on medical terms **141**

Acknowledgements **143**

Tea for Two: Friendship steeped in love **149**

INTRODUCTION

So, you've peed on a stick. This means you either think you're pregnant or you are. And if you are, in approximately nine months, that baby will come out. You will soon notice that mothers around you begin to impart their 'motherly' advice (whether you asked for it or not). But, somehow, that advice never extends to the specifics or realities of childbirth. Instead, you're reassured with platitudes of love and excitement (perhaps to avoid being scared off?). We all started out as a newborn baby. Someone, somehow birthed you. But do you know how you entered this world? What that experience was really like? Chances are, you have little to no idea how your mum did it. She just did. It is just the circle of life taking its natural course, right?

It's true that mummies have been having babies for a long, long time, and not too much has changed over this long, long time. It still can only be done by women. And it's safe to say because birth can only be performed by women that it was only ever seen as 'women's business'. Performed by women and traditionally managed by women. Of course, modern medicine has improved childbirth over the centuries, particularly in relation to the options around pain relief, caesarean sections and where you can birth your baby (for example, in a hospital, a birthing centre or a homebirth). But too much remains the same.

Why are so many babies and mothers still being harmed or, worse still, dying during childbirth? Why are some mums totally okay post-birth and others left with life-changing injuries and heartache? Why does childbirth still carry so many risks, especially given that we have become so advanced in understanding these risks? Every medical procedure carries a certain level of risk. Prior to any planned surgery, doctors make you sign that piece of paper saying they have explained everything regarding the procedure, along with the risks involved, in a separate appointment. But somehow vaginal childbirth seems to stand alone and not be the same category as a medical procedure. Why is that?

My gut feeling is because of one powerful word – 'natural'. Putting the word 'natural' before 'childbirth' swings the pendulum away from medical intervention and away from any discussion of the risks involved in vaginal births. Childbirth is seen by many as something women's bodies just know how to do naturally, and any shift away from this 'natural ideology' is then placed in opposition to this. In particular, having a caesarean section has somehow ended up being pitted against natural birth. When you hear the word 'natural' these days, you likely think of organic and pure, and as being better for you. And we all strive for what we are led to believe is better for ourselves and our babies.

One of the common questions I've been asked after becoming a mum is whether I went 'natural' or had a caesar. Like this matters because…? I don't know why this is a topic of conversation among mums. I've had other mothers actually say things like, 'Oh I tried natural, it failed, so I had to go for an emergency C-section'. And this was said in something more like a whisper, like it was something to be ashamed of. I always felt sad for mums who would hesitate or somehow feel ashamed of saying they had a caesarean. At the end of the day, it made no difference to my friendships with these women. But if I'm totally honest, at the time, being able to say I gave birth naturally did make me feel special – like I was somehow better for being able to do so.

Then one day I realised I was not special. And I wasn't actually part of that natural mothers' club either; that was a load of bullshit. There was nothing natural about my birth. Perhaps it progressed 'naturally' in the beginning when all was going well, but when shit got real, I had five or six more people (who I didn't know) enter the room with metal tools – and there is nothing natural about that. From that day on, I decided to call my birth was it really was: a traumatic instrumental vaginal birth.

The word 'vagina' is not an everyday word in average conversations. It has a private and sexual connotation to it, a taboo, that usually prevents it being spoken about unless you work in the medical field. The uneasy feeling it gives people has led to the belief that we don't talk about vaginas with the average Joe. You are not likely to discuss your vagina with your postie or dentist, let alone your dad or brother. And there lies part of the problem.

The number of women being affected by traumatic childbirth is immeasurable because so many women are still not able to talk about it. They don't report it. It is too private. How can people at the top, those writing the policies surrounding childbirth, ever know the damage being caused if it is not even spoken about? A problem isn't really a problem until enough people talk about it and these voices get louder and louder – that good old proverb of 'the squeaky wheel gets the grease'.

When I have shared my traumatic experience with the few women in my family I feel very close to, not one of them told me they felt this natural versus caesarean stigma existed when they birthed their babies years ago. They found it hard to understand what I was trying to say about feeling we were pushed into pushing, at whatever cost, and as if the 'natural' vaginal birth was the only way. None of them had any clue that this stigma stems in part from government policies such as 'Maternity: Towards normal birth in NSW'. This policy directive from 2010 led health professionals and mothers away from caesarean births and pushed for an increase in vaginal births – or, as they called them, 'natural childbirths'. Talk about galvanising this natural stereotype.

For expectant mothers receiving care under these kinds of policies, this natural childbirth ideology is what we are 'told and sold' from the very beginning.

Only during the research for this book did I discover the specific indicators that determine if your birth is normal or natural, neither of which simply mean vaginal over C-section. All along I thought I just had a failed natural or normal birth, but it turns out that's not the case. My first birth was not normal or natural. Just vaginal or instrumental – I think. And this is the whole point. I have never had anyone talk to me about my birth trauma, and no-one has ever explained what happened or what to call it. So I've been flying blind, going on what I thought. I had no idea, and I'm not alone here.

In the beginning ...

In the middle of the night in late January, I suddenly awoke with an indescribable feeling. There was a change within me. I can't really describe it, other than to call it a change, a fuzzy buzz in me. I sprung out of bed and went to the bottom of the bathroom vanity, where I had a secret stash of pregnancy tests. As I did so, I experienced a touch of deja vu.

Only the week before, I'd had the same feeling and done the same thing. I didn't share the disappointment with Tom about that negative pregnancy test. It was both confusing and hurtful because I thought the feeling I had was so real at the time. With the lingering negative test still in my mind, I hesitated for a minute – and then my bladder decided that while I was up, I might as well empty it. The gut feeling was no stronger this time, but 'curiosity killed the cat' kicked in.

I peed on the stick and waited while every second ticked over in what felt like slow motion. I had the stick face down. I wanted to

Introduction

'rip off the bandaid' in one go, and flip it over to reveal the answer. I could not sit and watch the two little lines develop (or not).

It turned out this test didn't show lines but instead had words – and mine said 'Pregnant 2–3 weeks'! Finally being able to turn the stick over and see the positive result was easily one of the most uncontrollably happy moments of my life. Overcome with joy, I took a photo of the test to prove that it was really happening and waited very patiently until 4:30 am to wake Tom and share our amazing news. We were having a baby! Finally a baby! He didn't react in the same way as me at first. It might have been the shock or just waking up. He was quiet. It was dark. Then I felt his smile when he was hit with the excitement oozing from me.

Even if I wanted to control my excitement, I couldn't. I was like a Cheshire cat with the worst-kept secret. I just wanted to shout it from the mountain tops. But you don't. No doubt you've heard about the 12-week rule – where you don't share your news in case you have a miscarriage. At first, we didn't really get the reasoning behind this unwritten law but thought we didn't want to jinx it (like telling people would change the outcome).

Becoming more aware of the fragility and vulnerability of this process left us wanting only the very best for our Little Ray of Sunshine. We were 'told and sold' on the ideology of natural child birth like it was the best option – or more so the one and only option, really.

We did all the things you're supposed to and waited until blood tests and the 12-week scan were completed before getting the green light to share our news. We read the pregnancy and childbirth books. Like deer in the headlights, we did the birthing classes. We did the birth plan. Ready, set, go! We were off. Eyes on the prize: that little baby. We wanted the right birth. The natural birth. The 'best' birth.

It was anything but those things. The birth of our baby was a traumatic experience, and it didn't need to be. In the hours and days following, we were so blissfully in love with our little baby that we didn't even know how significant the trauma was. We thought (and were made to believe by the hospital) that everything about my recovery was all normal. As educated people who are motivated by success, we now are left to wonder how we fell through the cracks and didn't see this coming. We didn't know what we didn't know.

What this book is for

My husband and I have learned so much in hindsight. We only wish we knew then half of what we know now. And that is where this book comes in. I've written this book to impart all the knowledge we have learned through our journey, in what can be the most vulnerable time for new parents. Through telling my story, this book questions this ideology of what natural means and how that is pitted against any medical advancements in the childbirth space.

This book also addresses the unspoken rule of 'secret women's business' and how the taboos around discussing the realities of birth are also based in fear of 'information overload' – that is, we are too scared of scaring first-time mothers with too many facts. The personal stories and anecdotes included here are designed to help you and not scare you. Looking back, I would have preferred to have been scared – and then moved through this fear – during the nine months of being pregnant, rather than feel a much greater level of fear as my legs were spread wide open and placed in stirrups while a doctor stood in front of me with surgical scissors.

I've included a chapter on my actual birth trauma in this book. A trigger warning will let you know this is the part when shit gets real. Again, I've included these details not to scare you, but simply to outline some of the things that can happen and do happen. More importantly, I've included my story to allow you to be better equipped in making the decisions needed at your time of need.

At the end of each chapter, I've also included some questions to help you think more about your own situation, and perhaps help you explore your own internal biases and assumptions.

Introduction

Throughout the process of creating this book, I asked myself who I was to be writing a book about childbirth. I'm not a doctor, a midwife or a doula and I am not medically trained in childbirth or childbirth psychology. And yet, I felt the societal expectation and pressure on me (simply because I'm female) that I should instinctively know how to birth a baby, and/or I should educate myself on how to manage my birth – as if it was my sole personal responsibility to learn all there is to know about this complex topic.

Don't get me wrong; I'm not saying all the available information should have been handed to me on a silver platter. I was happy to put in the effort to learn all I could. The point I'm trying to make here is that if you only ever have interactions with a one-sided view on childbirth, you will only ever know what you are 'told and sold'.

This complex and multifaceted topic invites very strong opinions and historical ideals. It seems that the two opposing camps of 'natural' (usually midwife-based care) versus 'medical' (obstetrician care) have moved so far apart that finding any sort of middle ground is too difficult. Proponents of each seem to need to defend their own ideologies and practices as being 'best practice' or 'gold standard' over the other. That we 'smart' humans are not able to have both what I call the 'woowoo' of childbirth and access to medical advancements to ensure babies and their mothers have the best chance of a positive outcome – for the both of them – seems so sad. Of course, I am talking in very general terms here. I know some obstetricians advocate for the best needs of their patients and some midwives do talk to their mothers about both birthing methods (with natural being the number one choice).

Importantly, I'm not anti-anything or pro-anything. I'm not here to change worldwide opinions and approaches to childbirth. I'm not trying to 'win' the argument one way or the other. I am simply a mumma who has felt caught in the middle. I've have birthed two babies and both experiences were very different. I also share my second birth experience with you – not as a way of putting it against the first, but to point out how knowing more rather than less made every bit the difference.

How you birth your baby should be up to you. Yes, you do have options and choices of how you get to that point of birthing. We can all be different and do things our own way. The fact remains, at the end of the day that baby is coming out via one of two ways: either through your vagina or through your tummy (C-section). Isn't it better to understand how both options can work by trying to remove some of the fear of the unknown – by knowing?

If you're pregnant while reading this, I hope by the end of this book you are able to get where you need to be about your own birth. I hope this book helps you feel informed and empowered to make decisions that are right for you now as you are pregnant, and throughout the birthing process. I hope you'll feel empowered to work out how to have conversations with your partner, family or friends (and how to deal with the overshare), and how to ask more questions from your healthcare provider and then to feel confident in the answers they provide.

While I don't pretend to be an expert and know everything about childbirth now, I have discovered a lot more information along the way. Sadly, I have also met too many other women who have had very similar experiences to me, and too many that are identical. To get the most out of this book, read each chapter sequentially to understand and know the process of how we even got here. And keep an open mind throughout this read and beyond. I've already mentioned the two teams that seem to be in the childbirthing arena – you are either all-natural or caesarean section. It doesn't need to be that way. Try to challenge your own thoughts and any biases you may have. Share what you learn from the book with your pregnant family and friends (who perhaps have just peed on that stick) or even your broken mummy friends with their broken vaginas.

And if you're a mumma who is still trying to fall pregnant, in some chapters later in the book you may feel like I should just be grateful for being able to fall pregnant in the first place. I am. I know how lucky I am to have been blessed with two babies. I don't take this process for granted for one minute. And I also do remember being on the other side and not fully understanding why other mummas could sometimes come across as not being 100 per cent grateful for their blessing. I get it.

If you are like me and it's too late – meaning you have already experienced birth trauma – I'm so very sorry. I'm sorry it happened to you. I'm sorry it happened to me.

Through the process of writing this book I have been able to find some resolve about what happened to me. I hope you can also take away something hopeful and positive for you.

Lastly, to those amazing professionals who work in this space and only ever have the best intentions for mummas and bubbas, thank you. I hope by reading this, you understand your power even more – the true sense of your power and level of trust mummas give you. Use it wisely. The time for change is now. We all need to be working together to better these outcomes for bubs and their mums.

CHAPTER 1
HOW DID WE GET HERE?

I always wanted to be a mumma bear. I love kids. That's why I became a teacher (and quickly found out kids are amazing to work with). Wanting my own baby was pretty much par for the course for me. It was always going to be part of my plan.

In late 2006, a visit to my lovely female GP to chat about planning for pregnancy ended up being anything but talking about a baby. I was 26, engaged and ready to be a wife and mumma. I had it all planned out: a big wedding, six kids and a big house. My first question was about what types of vitamins I needed to start taking. But our big dreams were quickly shattered. Towards the end of that baby-planning appointment, I asked my doctor to have a quick check of a lump near my collarbone. I almost didn't say anything, it was so small – like a pea-sized lump that felt similar to when I pulled a neck muscle at the gym. My doctor, however, immediately stopped baby talk, had a good feel around and was straight on the phone making urgent appointments for tests, scans, bloods and a biopsy.

In the week that followed, after all the invasive testing, my GP gave the blow of all blows. 'Stephanie, I'm sorry to say this, but you have

Hodgkin's lymphoma.' The next words I muttered (I can't remember verbatim) went something like, 'Yep, okay then. So when can I start trying to have a baby? How long do I have to wait before I can start trying?' Babies were our only focus, even more than the pending nuptials. 'No, Stephanie, you have cancer.'

Nothing about the next year or so that followed – surgery, chemo, radiation (and then picking up the pieces of the life and love I lost) – were part of my thought process. Let alone the struggles that can come from the treatments to keep you alive (which I plan to go into more detail in my next book *The C Word*).

Planning for in vitro fertilisation

Dealing with everything that followed that GP visit involved a steep learning curve, on many fronts. To take on the baby challenge, we were sent to an IVF specialist to talk about freezing eggs before chemo started. I was okay with this because it was reassuring to know that becoming a mummy would happen, but we might just need to wait the year out.

The first experience with the IVF clinic was horrendous. In my mind, we were going to sit in a consultation room with comfy lounge chairs and cheesy artworks. The nurses and doctors would explain how it all worked, and perhaps even throw a little sympathy our way because of why I was there in the first place.

Ah, no. From the clinic wait room (full of big bellies, which only added insult to injury), we were taken into what I can only describe as a broom closet. It literally had a mop and bucket, a few sterile trollies and some cupboards. The three of us could hardly fit. After I was asked to sit down to take bloods, I asked the nurse who was pulling the arm strap tight what the samples were for.

She muttered a few words and then it happened. I burst into tears, what the hell was this? It was nothing like I had imagined. Is this IVF? Wow, where was my 'woowoo'? (This is a term I've borrowed from an author friend, Tony.) By 'woowoo' I mean that feeling of warmth, care, nurture and love. Isn't having a baby all of those things? And I wasn't feeling any of them.

I think the nurse gave me a tissue and continued to draw out blood – as tears continued to fall down my face. When she was done, she gave me a black bag full of drugs to start taking over the next few days. As I left, I felt like I was carrying my dreams of being a mumma in that little black bag.

Arriving back to my fiancé's family home, I felt as if I needed to act excited that this was happening. Like this was all a good thing. My then mother-in-law cleared out her wine fridge and carefully placed the black bag inside. We all had a laugh that this must be a momentous occasion for her wine fridge to be cleared out to make way for the grandbaby. She then beautifully wrapped a little pink ribbon around the strap of the bag. I lost it, really lost it. Not at her or the ribbon. Everything else. I ugly cried for so long. It was all too much. Everything was wrong about what just happened. My woowoo was completely gone.

Over the next few days, things seemed to improve and get a little easier with the IVF process – until I received a phone call from my treating oncologist. He told me that I didn't have time for the IVF. My cycle was at the wrong end, and if I waited to complete the process, I could be dead. When I tried to ask questions, he cut me off with something like, 'Would you rather a baby or a baby with no mum?'

Okay, so by this stage I was up to the WTF?! Although, funnily enough, I didn't think too much about my own mortality – even though it was just put in front of my face. I wanted that baby so badly that it blurred my judgment. It wasn't until my fiancé pointed out the obvious – that leaving a newborn baby without a mummy was selfish – and then the decision was not one to really be made. It was just decided. No IVF.

All the same, I couldn't be the one to take the black bag with the little pink ribbon back to the clinic. It had to be someone – anyone – else. I wasn't about to give my dream back. So I put that in the too-hard basket (for someone else to deal with) and focused on getting to that next step and getting back on track. I just had to take care of a few things first.

The issue was that I knew what was coming – with the chemo, I mean. I knew what it was going to do to me. I'd sat with a mate throughout his cancer treatment only a few years earlier. And I'd watched it slowly 'kill' the person he was. I'd seen the needles, the pain, the sickness, the sometimes wishing he was dead. Fortnight after fortnight, I was there right beside him. That's not really something we can say we look forward to.

By now Christmas was fast approaching. I think my surgery was a couple of days out from Christmas Day, with chemo meant to start at the beginning of the new year. This didn't happen. I didn't start chemo until the end of January because my treating doctor went on holidays. My biggest frustration about all this was I would have had plenty of time to do that IVF cycle. And to add insult to injury, once the chemo had already started, my new haematologist told me that I had a good chance of survival and probably could have done the IVF if I'd really wanted to. Ouch, again!

Moving on and finding a new life

Like most people, I learned to move on from these things – although it happened pretty slowly for me. I did eventually recover physically but emotionally, it took its toll. There was nothing left of me. I had nothing left to give and I had no clue who I was or what I wanted in life. The door on the engagement and life I always dreamed of had closed. Skip forward a few years and life took a total different direction. Treatment was complete, and I'd received a clean bill of health at each yearly check-up. It was living time. I travelled and worked overseas. I found myself again. After feeling numb for a few years, I started to thaw out. The thoughts of becoming a mumma started flooding back.

I had found love again, this time with a familiar face. I had met Tom through mutual friends years ago. We reconnected and realised we wanted to be more than just friends. I now had the new love, new job and new home in a new town – and remembered that yearning feeling I'd had before. It was like a void in the pit of my heart (and my tummy) that I felt could only be filled with a baby growing inside me.

Not having been on the pill since chemo finishing, I suddenly realised it'd been a few years with no contraception. Although I remember thinking it was funny that I hadn't fallen pregnant yet, it wasn't anything I really talked about with anyone at the time. And it wasn't something I really thought long and hard about until I was married and still nothing. No changes. No bump.

So I started asking some questions (kind of 'in passing') of a friend of my bestie, Sharn. The friend worked at an IVF clinic in Sydney. I was still petrified by what happened last time, but she seemed really lovely, gentle and kind. So I shared what had happened to me at the other clinic and she painted a totally different picture for me. She offered for me to meet her boss and have a chat.

So Tom and I did. And, yes, it was totally that 'woowoo' I was looking for so many years ago. And it turned out things looked okay – meaning I wasn't facing any massive health hurdles when it came to being able to fall pregnant. An array of vitamins for both parents was prescribed and a minor day procedure for me was carried out (to what I can only describe as 'clear out my tubes'). The major thing I learnt during this was that each month women only have a 15 to 30 per cent chance of falling pregnant on their own. (As you likely know, female fertility declines with age. For women in their 20s, their chances of getting pregnant within one year are 78 to 86 per cent.) This surprised me a lot. I thought conception was just a given, and that it would happen 'naturally'.

A few further months went by and, with each period, I was feeling more and more disappointed. It was still early days but, even so, I asked the IVF specialist when I could make the next-step appointment to get started, if things didn't work naturally. And so the appointment was set for a Wednesday in January 2015. In the meantime, it was game on. Tom and I didn't really want to talk about getting pregnant day and night, at the risk that it would take the woowoo out of our relationship. We'd heard that IVF can feel mechanical, not overly romantic and certainly not 'natural'. But I was definitely focused on it.

I'm sure you (and many, many women) can relate to that heart-sinking feeling you get when you have waited the two minutes (watching every second pass by) before you can flip that stick over – anticipating a 'double line' or a plus sign – only to see a minus sign, a single line. You double-check the back of the box, hoping against hope you've made a mistake. *Was I meant to wait two minutes or three? Have I flipped it too soon? Did I not pee right? Maybe it's because it wasn't the start of the day wee?* You scan over the FAQs to see if you have done everything right. You give the stick a shake just in case it is still processing. You examine that single line one more time, hoping it has changed its mind. But nope, it hasn't. You are not pregnant. (These days it actually says NOT pregnant, just to make things super clear.) It was a big ouch moment for me each time.

I would quickly shove the negative test and its wrapping back into the box and discreetly throw it in the bin. I didn't want anyone to know. I'm not sure why, but I never told Tom about any of the negative tests. Maybe it was too hard or too sad. I also didn't share any of this with any family or friends. Maybe it's because of that 'secret women's business' code that prevents us from talking about the long and sometimes very painful journey to becoming a mum.

By the start of January, I was starting to mentally prepare for my appointment to start IVF. I also threw myself into work as a distraction, which was easy because it was the start of a new school year, at a new school.

This particular Monday night I was staying with Sharn. She'd been diagnosed with motor neurone disease a couple of years back. Her husband was working the night shift, so it was a sleepover for the girls. We had a great night. It was only as it came time to sleep that I shared with her my heartache about not being pregnant.

That very morning I'd had another message on the stick telling me I wasn't pregnant. We both had a little tear and then fell asleep. This was the first time I opened up to someone. Sharn is someone I trust with my life. This was a big thing.

On the Wednesday of the following week was my scheduled appointment to start the IVF process. On the Monday of that week, I had my early morning awakening and saw that 'Pregnant 2–3 weeks' staring back at me. The call I then had to make to the IVF clinic was the happiest call I'd had to make in a long time. Funnily enough, the lady on the phone said they often received similar calls just prior to appointments. This second experience with IVF was very different. The interactions were both professional and loving.

So here we were. Finally pregnant and very much looking forward to rubbing my bump like I was a lucky Buddha, weird food cravings (just like in the movies), shopping for tiny clothes and being a mumma. The hard part was done. The fun was about to start ... right?

Ask yourself ...

- Have you ever visited an IVF clinic, or been through IVF treatment? How did the clinic make you feel (woowoo or boohoo)? How did the experience make you feel about your body and your ability to become pregnant? Did you start to feel like your body had failed you and you needed to shift your trust to outside 'experts'?

- Have you experienced the sorrow of a negative pregnancy test? Did you tell anyone about it, or feel like you had to wait until the joy of a positive one?

- If you have a partner, did you discuss any of your feelings about getting pregnant with them?

CHAPTER 2
PRE-BIRTH – A BUN IN THE OVEN

prenatal – a term meaning 'before birth'
(alternative terms are 'antenatal' and 'antepartum')

As soon as we found out we were pregnant, we quickly entered a whole new world of terminology. We had all these new words to remember, including ones that didn't seem to make sense, such as antenatal. How can *prenatal* mean the same as *antenatal*? Antenatal sounds like it should be used at a different stage, after the job is done, not at the beginning.

From that very moment of peeing on that stick and seeing the result, I started writing letters to our little one. Over the next few weeks I described every overwhelming, loving feeling I was having. It was such a privilege and I was very proud. The medical side of things was just a sidenote really. It was all about the 'woowoo' and love for this baby.

My local GP at the time was also very happy for us. He wanted to return home to London at some point and also start a family with his partner. He had not long been in Australia and was new to our local area, so hadn't been here long enough to know the system or doctors very well. He simply completed the standard referral for our local public hospital. At the time, we had no idea what it all meant but in the referral, my GP had circled 'high risk'. We didn't pay attention to it at the time – and, as it turned out, neither did anyone else.

Entering the public hospital system

It is hard to forget the very first appointment at the hospital. It was for 3.30 pm. This was the latest time you could 'request'. (It was really a case of you get what you get.) I had to leave work early because school didn't finish until 3.25 pm and it was at least one hour travel time to get back home and then to the hospital. I shared the news with my boss at the time, and he congratulated me and seemed supportive. He let me leave early that day. (This is certainly not how this part of the story ends, but more on that a bit later.)

Tom and I arrived early for the appointment. We sat in the waiting room full of mummas at all stages – women with full bellies and little bellies, women with kids already – and, my goodness, the room was full. Not a spare seat in sight. We waited and we waited. It was 6 pm before our names were called. The whole experience felt like we were in a cattle station, going along with the herd. 'Next, next … next!'

We (finally) met with a doctor, and can't even remember who it was or really what we spoke about. All I do remember is that the chat was very quick. We were in and out in five minutes or so, and left more confused than when we went in. We certainly didn't love it – and there was certainly no woowoo there. Looking back, it did feel like we were boxed into that category of standard 'first-time parent nerves' and not taken too seriously. We felt rushed in and out, like it was a cookie-cutter appointment – same questions, same answers, and no real opportunity to discuss anything. Certainly, we did not discuss any risk factors or me being in a high-risk category. We actually had no clue why I was classed as 'high risk' or what that might have meant for my pregnancy or birth. We were just told what the next steps were – booking more appointments.

By now we were past the 12-week mark (and also past the informal announcement freeze), so we could start sharing our wonderful news. Not loving our first hospital experience, we started asking friends and other people about what they did. We also started reading forums online and within parent groups on Facebook. I started to feel a strong sense of a public versus private hospital debate, with some seeing going private as accessing a better level of care, with more autonomy. This included discussions about the private system being more willing to allow mums to have a choice about their birthing method. But this was also met with a lot of backlash from the public hospital advocates about women 'choosing' a C-section and the whole 'too posh to push' thing – I was already seeing the judgements and side-taking! I sensed a defensiveness on the side of the supporters of the public system (and as a public servant of many years in the education system, I also wanted to defend the system that is there to support everyone). However, these forums made the private system sound so much better for us. It seemed able to provide a better level of personalised care. And given my past history during my cancer treatment – with the lack of continuity of care and the frustration that caused – Tom and I decided we'd prefer to go private, remembering we only wanted the very best.

No luck there, however. When I phoned the private hospital to see what I needed to do next (because no-one told us), they said I needed to double-check my level of cover prior to making any appointments. When I checked the coverage I'd held since becoming a teacher, I disappointedly discovered that it didn't cover me for obstetrics. Over a decade of private health cover and I'd had no clue that I didn't tick the right box all those years ago. What young 20 year-old would? I'm pretty sure that I wouldn't have even been across the word 'obstetrics' at that age.

Anyway it wasn't to be, so onto plan B. How do we get the best care with what we had access to? We decided to chat with our neighbours, who had just had their second baby girl. They told us about a special program offered by the local public hospital, run and managed by the midwives. I tracked down an application form for the program and found this was their opening paragraph:

> *We can offer you care by a midwife through pregnancy, birth and two weeks after birth. Our care focuses on your needs and those of your baby. Active labour, normal birth, breastfeeding and early discharge home from the Birthing Unit are important to us. We have limited places available and priority is given to women having their first baby.*

You can probably see why we found this so appealing. It sounds so lovely! All natural and normal, and the ideal way to welcome your baby into this world. The woowoo. It even says 'normal birth'. At the time I read 'normal birth' I thought it sounded funny because I don't think anyone would ever request an 'abnormal birth'.

Our neighbour told us most women phoned the program to get on their waiting list as soon as they'd peed on a stick. And yes, they were so right. When I phoned saying I was approximately 12 weeks, they said they were already full. Bugger.

Troubles with the boss man

By this stage, I also needed to go to a few more hospital appointments because I'd been diagnosed with gestational diabetes from the very first blood tests. To get to these appointments, I needed to leave work early or have the day to attend compulsory education to be able to self-manage the blood sugar testing (six times a day) and learn about the special diet with the hope I wouldn't need medication. My boss wasn't too happy about this and soon had no problem telling me so. His words were something along the lines of, 'You're not the first woman to have a baby, you know, and I'm not sure I can approve your sick leave – as you're not really sick.'

This type of behaviour spiralled out of control over a very short period. I wasn't expecting it to get as bad as it did. He became very bitter and our longstanding collegial relationship didn't mean anything. As you can imagine, the whole situation caused a lot of stress, to the point of daily nose bleeds. Before this, I'd never really understood what women meant when they talked about sexual discrimination, because I'd never experienced it. Until now. I decided I needed to be living differently from this. This was not a way to be each day, and my baby needed to come first. I quickly learnt that I could not change his thoughts on this or change him, so I needed to change the situation.

More than ever, I felt like I needed to be part of the midwife-led program. Their appointments were after hours, you met your personal midwife and her backup midwife, and only saw either one of them. Continuity of care was provided all the way until the birth and beyond, with at least one of the team helping you birth your baby and then sharing the care between them at home afterwards. Along with all the great benefits, I also wouldn't need to ask for any more time away from work.

So I became even more determined. I phoned a few times to ask more questions about the waitlist and explained how I not only *wanted*, but *needed* this program. I was a few mummas down the waitlist and was told it didn't look promising. Luckily this was around the time things started to settle at work as all the initial appointments were done.

A midwife then phoned me late one afternoon saying that a mumma had just been 'kicked off' the program. This meant a spot had come up and if I could attend an appointment at 7 pm the following day, I could have a chance of being accepted. Yes, yes, yes. In my mind I was already at that appointment to be interviewed for this special program (and was happily ignoring those loaded terms 'kicked off' versus 'being accepted').

Walking through the hospital at 7 pm on a Friday night, with no-one really around, felt strange. The Antenatal Unit wait room was a ghost town. The only two people there were my midwife and a cleaner. My midwife was all dressed up about to go out for a farewell dinner, and I felt bad that she was missing the start of the dinner to see me.

She reassured me it was okay and proceeded with the (long) appointment, including lots of questions for the midwife and from the midwife. A full family medical and mental health history were taken. Lots of questions (including about my cancer and even about whether anyone in my or Tom's family suffered from anxiety or depression) but no explanation of what my answers might mean and how they might be connected to my level of care or affect my birth. She then explained the process to me in a very woowoo kind of way. It all sounded just as expected – beautiful, supportive, natural and somewhat easy. I left that appointment on cloud nine.

Hello – you're in!

Now the only thing left was for me to be accepted. And then I was. That call of acceptance was wonderful. I felt special, like I was now part of a special group, receiving special attention. I feel like I had a bit of an unspoken higher status thing. All our appointments were made afterhours at a time and day that worked for us. When we arrived and sat in the wait room, we only waited (at most) five minutes before our names were called – leaving everyone else (who had been waiting much longer) to continue to wait for their 'next, next' appointment.

We only met with our first midwife briefly one more time before being informed that she was leaving to 'continue her studies'. We later found out that she too was 'kicked off' the program for not being skilled enough. At the time, we felt like we may have dodged a bullet. We wanted someone who knew exactly what they were doing and had lots of experience – because some early fears were starting to present themselves.

I'm sure that many – if not all – mummas experience some level of fear when it comes to pregnancy, childbirth and motherhood. This fear manifests in different ways, and about different parts of their journey to motherhood. Although pinning down exactly what there is to be fearful of can be difficult. And I'm sure it is different for different mummas, too. For me, it was the unknown that was scary. Not knowing what exactly was coming. Not being able to predict and 'fix'. Fixing things is how I processed fear in the past, and it had worked for me so far!

If I'm honest, the fear of not meeting my little baby was the scariest thing. While most people only talk about the good parts of pregnancy and birth, there is always someone with one of those horrible stories – about their friend of a friend who lost their baby during childbirth. Those stories are scary. I only ever thought about my baby. That feeling of needing to protect my baby was intense.

This feeling to protect my baby forced me to leave work early – along with feeling very awkward taking my bloods three times a day in a storeroom, while my six-year-old students read books. The pressure from boss man continued to the point of harassment. We were not really on talking terms and I avoided his power trip conversations as much as possible. He then started doing strange passive-aggressive things like coming into my classroom every day and just sitting up the back. He'd say nothing – not even as much as a hello – and then walk out.

At the time I was on a temporary contract (having started at this new school at the start of the year) and one day at the end of lunch, with the entire school present, he whispered quietly to me that he was going to have to terminate my contract before I went on maternity leave. He gave some longwinded reason about me still being permanently attached to another school. From that moment, I made the decision not to get caught up in his issues about me being pregnant and I left it to the people in higher places to deal with him.

Keep calm and baby will grow

This was the time to focus on this pregnancy and my little baby. So that is what I did. I spent all my time and energy on making sure I was on top of my diet and exercise to manage the gestational diabetes, because I had been told that babies born from mums with this can be much bigger and grow a lot towards the end of pregnancy. During that initial appointment with my first midwife, I had asked about the best child birthing classes to go to. She recommended a private provider whose main focus was to keep calm. So I went about enrolling Tom and I into these classes. They were taught over a weekend, so we made the most of it and travelled about an hour south for a lovely weekend away.

Our calm birthing classes were taught in a very relaxed setting (in a midwife's home) with three or four other couples all wanting the same thing – a lovely natural birth. It felt more like a meditation weekend compared to those birthing classes you see on TV, where everyone is sitting in a circle on a bouncy ball doing heavy breathing. We left with a workbook, a flash drive filled with meditations (that I actually did do) and the idea that I would be 'breathing this baby down'. No talk of contractions – instead they were called 'surges' that 'let you know baby is ready'. The whole experience painted the picture of romance and love, and we were 100 per cent sold on this ideal.

By this time, we had been introduced to a new midwife, and then another one, who was the last stop. She was the one who was going to be with us for this last part of the pregnancy journey, birthing and beyond. She had great credentials, along with four children of her own. She spoke confidently with a big warm smile that made us feel at ease.

We took our list of questions to each appointment. They were always focused solely on the baby. What was going to be the absolute best for this baby? We always wanted to know about something. What about this? And what if that? Sometimes we could feel our midwife's frustration with being asked questions. The responses started sounding the same: 'you'll be fine' and 'stop worrying'. I always felt this underlying fear of being 'kicked off' the program so I was conscious of the number of questions we had and of picking the right time during the appointment to ask. I started being what I now would call 'the good patient', including not asking too many questions and going to pre-natal yoga to be calm.

To get the ongoing answers I was looking for (without bombarding our midwife) I read pregnancy books and forums online. I think *Up the Duff* by Kaz Cooke was still all the rage, even though it had been around for a long time. It took a look into the funny side of pregnancy, and I thought this might be helpful, take the edge off a bit. I read a few other pregnancy books – usually the ones with the dreamy mumma wearing all white on the cover, naturally looking beautiful, big smiles while gently embracing her bump. How lovely. I loved that too.

We also attended the midwife program's birthing class. The entire midwife team were present, so we got to meet them all (so we would be comfortable with someone else if on the day of our bubba arriving our main midwife wasn't available).

Feeling the woowoo

It was circle time in this class, just minus the heavy breathing. All the mummas and their partners sat together in a circle while the head midwife gave her talk. I only remember bits and pieces of her talk now, but the overall focus was on how the midwife program came about and how we should be promoting it to keep it going.

What I will never forget is how I felt when they introduced a new mumma, her husband and their newborn baby girl. I think she was only a few days old. In they walked, with bub in a pouch, tucked in all snug and warm on mumma's chest.

The first-time parents looked so in love. With big smiles, they spoke of their birthing experience with the midwife program. It all sounded so romantic – no drugs or pain meds, and a three-hour birth. They were so grateful for their midwife. As mumma spoke to the group, she ever so gently patted her bub in the pouch, one hand on her little back and the other on her little bottom. I remember her doing this alternate rhythm with each hand. I wanted that! That exact thing. We'd even purchased a baby pouch similar to that one. The entire time, bub didn't make a sound.

Both birth class experiences matched. They told the same story. The key messages were to be calm, trust the midwife and breathe the baby down. We had a few things for homework, including making a playlist of all the songs we liked for birth, finding the scent we liked and having it ready for the birthing suite diffuser, and buying a yoga mat and exercise ball to bring with us and pack a bag ready for hospital.

Our calm birthing classes also emailed us a birthing plan. This was a pre-filled, one-page form that both parents signed and gave to our midwife team. We were able to add one or two things into the plan that we felt suited us, one of which was not to have anyone else in the delivery suite. This message came from both the calming birthing classes and midwife-led program, with the idea behind it communicated along the lines of, 'Only you two made the baby, so you really only need you two (and midwife) to birth the baby'. That romantic ideal made sense to us.

This didn't make sense to my mum, and she had a really hard time trying to understand why I wouldn't possibly need her in the room. I think Mum took it as me not *wanting* her in the room. She was there for my sister's two births and her own sister's four births, so she'd just assumed she would be there for mine. This did cause a bit of heartache between us all leading up to the birth, but our midwives' advice at the time was not to worry too much and that Mum would 'get over it' when she was holding her grandchild.

The level of trust between our midwife, Tom and me was compelling. Essentially we trusted our midwife with our baby's life (we never considered we'd need to think about trusting her with my life). The need for that level of trust was immense and that need only continued to grow. There was nothing more important than the little 'us' we were about to deliver.

We were ready to go. The countdown was on.

> **Ask yourself ...**
>
> - How aware are you of the opposing sides that seem to form in discussions about childbirth? How do you feel about private versus public care, for example, or about midwife versus obstetric care? How caught up do you become in these debates surrounding vaginal versus C-section births?
>
> - Even if you're not yet pregnant, have you been in a situation where you felt you knew so little (and the stakes seemed so high) you had to put all your faith in the 'experts' advising you? If you haven't yet experienced such a situation, what does this tell you about the pregnancy and birth experience?

CHAPTER 3
THE BIRTH – BAKING DAY

Trigger warning: parts of this chapter talk about trauma during my labour.

Bake a cake, they say. Perhaps you've already heard this little piece of birthing advice, and during the midwife-led birthing class they repeated it: when you think you are in labour, stay home and bake a cake to focus your mind on something else (and just let your body do its thing). So I did. Luckily for me at the time I had family holidaying close by and it was my uncle's birthday, so it was fitting that I made a cake for him.

The weeks leading up to 'baking the cake' were torturous – because I was so excited to meet my baby. I was getting impatient. Like for most first-time mummas, every twitch, movement or slight cramp felt like, 'This is it! Quick, get the bag and let's go'. To speed things along, I tried walking up and down stairs, eating curry and having smoothies with pitted dates (which apparently helps get things moving south). I even started setting deadlines for bub. I thought to myself, *Okay, baby, tomorrow is 15/10/15. I like the symmetry. A good day to be born, hey? So come on, then.*

Baby didn't listen, and 15/10/15 came and went. The official due date was around 17/10/15, and that came and went, too. Once we got to 19/10/15, the worry crept in. *I'm now 'overdue'. I'm now over the 40 weeks. This can't be good, right?* The last scan at 36 weeks showed that bub was already big. I felt big. I was big. There seemed no way my tummy could grow outwards anymore. I went to sleep each night thinking, hoping, I would wake up in a pool of water from my waters breaking during my sleep (I even went as far as placing a toddler 'wet-the-bed' mat under my sheets).

On Monday morning Tom left for work as normal, but with the clear idea that he could be called home any second because of how past my due date I was. I cleaned up the house and started to feel what I can only describe as a tingle. I felt a bit off, too. I was meant to meet my family for lunch but had this sense that something was going to happen and I didn't want to put myself in a situation where I wasn't able to follow the birthing plan. So it was time to get baking.

I phoned our midwife and told her that I was baking a cake. Her instructions were to stay home as long as I could and to phone the hospital (not to go in) when I felt I just couldn't take it anymore. While the cake was cooling, I phoned Tom to come home. Things were starting to heat up down there.

He continued to work from home on his laptop while I watched TV – well, kind of watched. I was on my yoga mat stretching and breathing through the movements. The feelings down there continued to get stronger and stronger. By the early afternoon we called the hospital and were told we could come in to be checked if we wanted to. After a quick check up, however, I was told that I was only 1 cm dilated and to go home.

Back home...

Time to bring out the exercise ball. It felt like I bounced the afternoon away. At dinner time I couldn't eat anything – partly because

The birth – baking day

I was too busy focused on the job at hand and also because I had that fear of pooing on my baby during the delivery.

After dinner time and into the night I did what we had learnt and used the shower to relax and moved through each surge. It was now time for the big guns: the bath. Over the next few hours I was in and out of the bath and shower. We were going great. The only thing worried at this point was the cat. He didn't like the noises coming from me.

No way were we going to bed that night. We stayed in the lounge room with dimmed lights and quiet background noise. The pain kept building until the shower and bath stopped working. The pain was too intense.

We had my bestie Sharn's husband on standby to drive us into the hospital. We called him quite late and drove back to the hospital, arriving at around 11 pm. It was exciting. I had a gut feeling we were not going to be turned away this time. Our midwife examined me and said 'Well done, Steph. You are 7 cm dilated and will be meeting your baby tonight.' Wow! The thrill of knowing we did all that work at home. So awesome.

We said goodbye to our friend who drove us in and were shown into the birthing suite. It was kind of like checking into a hotel. We had our own room and bath. The lights were down low, music on. How romantic. We were beyond excited.

We wanted it all to be right. Tom set up the snacks while I turned on the oil diffuser. Setting up was fun. It was a good distraction from the rumbles in my belly, which were getting stronger and stronger. Our midwife sat very quietly in the corner of the room, looking like she was doing some type of paperwork, letting us do our own thing. It was really nice.

As things started to become more intense, our midwife asked if I wanted to jump in the bath. Sure, why not. I remember Tom and I having a little giggle about how easy it all was. We didn't really understand what all the fuss was about in the movies. I certainly wasn't sweating profusely and screaming that I hate him for 'doing this to me'. I also had this little secret thought inside my head – that I was super tough and had been through a lot worse than this. Only this time my reward was going to be much greater. Meeting my baby was the only thing on my mind.

Time then seemed to stand still. The anticipation was building, as were the tummy rumbles. I'd say they were definitely 'surges' by now (in medical terms, they are called 'contractions'). I rode through each one, knowing they would eventually pass, knowing each one meant that baby was that much closer to sliding on out. Only Tom and I were still in the quiet room, moving through each one. I could not get comfy on the bed so I walked around a lot.

I became tired. It was well into the early morning and I was tired from walking around. Our midwife asked me to hop onto the bed so she could examine me. She asked if she could break my waters. This was a tricky question that I didn't know how to answer. Our calm birthing classes and plan said not to let anyone 'rush' you. They informed us that hospitals have you on the clock. They like to keep things moving. At the time, I had the impression this was because they were so busy and just wanted to get people in and babies out. I didn't think this clock-watching might have anything to do with risk.

Our midwife gave me encouragement that I had already done great work on my own. I was now fully dilated but it was time to keep things moving along. I trusted her. She was the expert, not me. So I let her break my waters. Still nothing. More time passed and I was very sleepy. I wanted to sleep but just could not sit or lie down, because I had too much pain in my back and backside. Standing was the only tolerable position. My midwife also suggested keeping the fluids up because I was becoming dehydrated.

Good old Gatorade. Well, if it was good enough for me as an athlete, surely it could help here too. A few sips at a time were all I could take in. Then the body decided even that was too much and I began vomiting red Gatorade all over the bed. I remember feeling so sorry for making the mess and trying to help clean it up.

Moving things along

Our midwife took over and cleaned up. She told me that she was aware of my birth plan and not wanting to be cannulated because of my fear of needles (stemming back from chemotherapy) but that it needed to happen to keep things moving now that I was getting physically tired. My legs were uncontrollably shaking. I was hunched over the side of the bed trying to breathe and do all of the rocking movements I was taught. Tom was trying to calmly stroke my back while giving me all the encouragement I needed. As the contractions were getting stronger, so was his stroking. Some were harder than the actual contractions.

Again, I agreed with my midwife's advice, so it was time to lay down for the cannula, which was problematic for two reasons. Firstly, because it was so painful lying on my back and, secondly, because I knew they would not be able to easily get a vein. My veins were shot due to chemo. I tried telling them to do the right arm. Nope, they did the left and missed. We almost lost Tom once that blood shot up into the air and landed all over the bed. The nurse got a chair for him. Try again. Right side this time and got it in. Funny that!

Not long after the drip went in, shit got real. I mean, really real. No more laughing about the movies. This was that sweaty, screaming stage (although I never told Tom I hated him – he was amazing). By now we had gone from candles, music and just the three of us to a few different people coming in and out of the room. Some I was introduced to, some not.

Now I was back on my feet, hunched back over the bed. Our midwife's boss lady had also joined. I'd met her at the birthing classes, and knew she founded the program so must know what she was doing, too. She was wearing some type of gimmicky tee-shirt and looked nothing like the other hospital staff in uniform. Her reassuring voice was telling me to hold tight to this rubber band thing she tied to the other side of the bed. Our midwife was standing closely behind me with her hands squeezing my hips. Tom was right there beside me, still being the best cheerleader.

'Push...push...puuuush, Stephanie,' they were all saying. Importantly, I thought I was doing what they asked but I NEVER felt an urge to push. When I thought I was pushing, it didn't seem to feel any different. The pressure (not so much pain) was intense. I felt constipated. Like I was blocked without being able to release the pressure.

Other people (I'm guessing doctors and nurses) were still coming and going from the room. This next part felt like it all happened so suddenly (and I will never know exactly how long it was because it was never documented). I was back lying on the bed, my feet up in those stirrups (just like the movies), and legs wide open. Our midwife was on my right with Tom next to her and her boss lady on my left. Someone else was standing off to the right for the baby. Then in walked the registrar. She told me her name and that she was there to get baby out.

My immediate thought was something was wrong with baby. *Quick, help baby come out*, I thought. *I don't want anything happening to the baby.* The registrar told me my baby was posterior, and was facing the wrong way. At that very moment, I could not comprehend what she meant. Although, looking back, we remember being told at a scan that baby was facing posterior and we should try and have it turned. We also remember being dismissed very quickly by the midwife when we shared this information with her. And we did, in fact, see a doula for a massage technique that was meant to help turn the baby.

By this stage, the registrar was holding up something that looked like a cup, saying she needed to turn baby the right way, telling me what she was holding was like a vacuum. I looked directly into Tom's eyes. He could see the terror on my face, because he too looked the same. He then looked to our midwife for help.

Our midwife gave us both this slight nod. We all knew what it meant: let the registrar do what was needed. Even if it wasn't part of

The birth – baking day

the plan. At the same time, the registrar said to us that if she wasn't able to get baby out with the vacuum and a 'slight cut', I would be rushed off for an emergency C-section. The image of her pointing to the door with the scissors in her hand will be etched in my memory forever.

The idea of a C-section after all this was beyond me. It felt like a failure.

The registrar also seemed to have it all under control. A 'slight cut' and vacuum, and baby would be here. Not quite.

(This next part is based on more recent discoveries because we had no idea at the time or even after the birth. We only found out the following information while looking through records with a legal team).

Baby was stuck. The vacuum failed to turn baby the right way. The next vacuum failed too, as did the next one. The fourth vacuum also failed. The 'slight cut' (episiotomy) was actually a huge cut from the front to back. Meaning I was cut open from the opening of my vagina up towards the anus. It was shear agony. The pain in my heart was the most agonising part. I didn't think I was ever going to meet my little baby girl.

At this stage, it actually felt like the registrar was trying to shove baby back up, the wrong way. It was chaotic. Pain and pressure at the same time. It's very difficult to describe the feeling in words. (Even writing about it now, my body is having a physical reaction just thinking of that very moment.) I felt like my insides were being ripped from me. We now know it was the forceps being used to 'force' their way in and around baby. To get her out.

Then it was the most indescribable feeling of release. The pressure release was like the bottom of a bucket bursting from too much water. Everything came gushing out. I feel like there was nothing left inside me. Nothing at all. I felt very hollow.

Here she is ...

That all didn't matter now. My baby girl was on my chest. I was in shock. I kept asking if she was okay, if she was alive. It was only once she started squawking that I was relieved. My baby girl and I were meeting for the first time, on the outside.

I was finally a mumma bear. And I was so in love.

The cord was quickly cut and they took our little girl away. This only brought all the fear (and more) back that she was not okay. It was in our pre-filled birth plan to 'delay cord clamping'. We were told in our birthing classes that it was best for baby to lay there on mumma's chest as long as possible before clamping and cutting, until all the blood had drained from the cord. At the same time, the registrar stayed focused on my vagina. She told me it needed 'a bit' of stitching. My focus was on our baby girl. I couldn't take my eyes off her. Finally, the midwife placed baby back on my chest, wrapped in a blanket.

Well, hello there, little Elsie. Time stopped. The registrar was there for some time more, but by this stage I was numb down there anyway, and completely focused on Elsie.

Once all the stitching-up was finished (because a lot of repair work was actually required), the registrar vanished – never to be seen again. The midwives got me up out of bed and straight into the shower. Elsie got to meet her daddy and have skin to skin with him. I was showered, dressed and taken to the ward. I had lost a lot of blood during the birth and again in the shower, so they took me into the maternity ward in a wheelchair.

Elsie was born at 10.27 am. We were all tired. My eyes could not close, though. I couldn't stop looking at her. She was quiet and sleeping. Tom was sleepy, too. My body was sleepy but not my eyes. We were left to our own devices. The ward was very busy and noisy. I remember being frustrated with the loud talking from staff and other parents. I didn't want them to wake Elsie.

The birth – baking day

I was hungry. I called the nurses – and not just for that. I was so unsure of everything. All the books I'd read and all the birthing classes just don't prepare you for the amount of worry you have. *She is bubbling from the mouth, does that mean something? Her feet are red and sweaty, does that mean something? She is crying again and I've done all the checks of wet nappy, hungry, etc., so does that mean something?*

I'm sure most maternity ward nurse are pretty used to first-time mummas and all their questions – although I will say that some nurses were more helpful and some more dismissive then others. Tom had gone home to try to grab a few hours of sleep. I was hungry. I asked about lunch because I could smell and hear other people eating.

I was told to go and check on the food trolley at the back of the ward. I could hardly walk. When I got down there (with Elsie in the crib thingy), all the meals were gone. The one or two left were half-eaten ones. I let the nurse know and she said because of the timing of my birth, they wouldn't have had time to get my lunch order in and that I would need to wait until dinner service. I phoned Tom and he came back with some food for me (at least it was nice to be able to have a Maccas thick shake again) while the two of us sat watching Elsie just sleep and sleep some more.

Dads were not allowed to stay in the hospital I was at so Tom was sent home. I was very emotional as he left, probably because of being so tired, and also because I was going to miss him. We hadn't really spent any time apart since being pregnant. And it was a terrible night. There also was no dinner for me that night. I was feeding Elsie and got to the food trolley too late. All the meals were gone, again.

The family next to us had had a baby that day, too. Their baby screamed the whole night through. *Poor parents*, I was thinking. Elsie was crying too, but not as badly, and I thought it was only because of the baby next door. I was up and down like a yo-yo anyway. I could not control any part of my bladder or bowel. I kept getting up for the loo, but never quite making it.

The next day I was visited by our midwife's boss lady. At the time I thought that was very sweet of her to just call in to see how I was doing. I told her about my night of no sleep or food and she suggested I could rest better at home. Our midwife was scheduled to visit us at home every day for the next ten days anyway, so it seemed to make sense. Home it was then.

Home sweet home

I told the nursing staff that I was part of the midwife program and had been told I would recover and bond with my baby better at home. Before we could leave, they needed to first complete all of Elsie's checks and her hearing test. After lunch the necessary doctors were able to see her, and she was all cleared to go home. Not one nurse or doctor spoke to me about how I was doing or feeling before leaving. A nurse had asked me that morning if I was able to go to the toilet and I told her I was literally shitting myself, without even knowing. They gave me some more massive pad/nappy things and told me where the ice packs were located. (I bet Tom never thought he'd be taking two of his girls home in nappies.)

Before we left I asked the paediatric doctor about Elsie's crying. She had been crying all day long, and I couldn't keep blaming the baby next door. The doctor said her head probably hurt – that she had been through a lot and that bump on her head would be sore. They prescribed her some Panadol – yes, at one day old.

That 'bump' they were talking about was a red and bloodied circle shape on the back of her head. For a little while they were concerned it was 'boggy', meaning not good. No-one ever really explained how it got there or what it meant. This was the start of the 'it's all normal' phenomenon. (Not so normal, of course, when almost four years on the bones on her head still have the circle imprint from the vacuum. But the not so normal was only beginning.)

Ask yourself ...

- What was your image of how labour and birth should look, either before giving birth or reading this chapter? How much did you think 'Hollywood' birth matched up to the reality? How much did you *want* to know about the reality?

- What did you previously know about maternal trauma and death rates during birth? Or did you assume (like me) these just didn't happen in modern hospitals, in this day and age?

- If this chapter reflects some of your own birth trauma, I'm so sorry for what you have gone through. How much can you relate to? Where does your story differ?

CHAPTER 4
AFTER BIRTH

After Elsie getting the 'all clear', we signed some paperwork and, without so much as a goodbye, walked ourselves out of the maternity ward around 8.30 pm. I felt faint and weak but passed it off as just being nervous about taking this precious little human out in the big wide world. It was raining and cold, which was odd for that time of year. We ever so carefully drove our little girl home – me sitting next to her in the back holding her hand, Tom driving about 20 kilometres per hour.

Back at home we placed our sleepy princess in her bassinet, and looked at each other with 'now what' kinds of faces? It was a strange feeling. If baby is sleeping, what do parents do? What were those 'parenty' type things that parents do now, the things we read about in the books?

We didn't need to think too hard. Elsie told us what we needed to do – well, actually more *when* something needed to be done, not *what*. The crying told us something, but we had no clue what, really. We learnt along the way, through a process of elimination – check for wet nappy, hungry, cold, hot, tired. Repeat. Being new parents alone was stressful. Trying to get it right was stressful. We just wanted her to be okay. The confusion about what her crying meant was hard. I thought that if I couldn't fix her – that is, stop her crying – I wasn't being a 'good' mum. I made judgements about my parenting based on her level of crying.

I was also stressed, personally – and silently. I was in pain. It took a day or two for all the pain medications I was having in hospital to wear off, and the first few days I was so swollen it was all still numb down there. But then all the pain hit, I could not sit down for weeks following child birth. Not at all. I was just so happy to be a mumma and be home with my baby that I didn't want it to matter. It did start to matter, though. I could not sit to breastfeed Elsie or sit to do anything. It was too painful from front to back. Lying down was the only position I could be in that would lessen the pain. I started to let our midwife know about the troubles I was having, and she suggested things like sitting on a rolled-up towel. I tried other things suggested too, like sitting on a doughnut cushion, but nothing really seemed to relieve the pain; it just made it worse. Not even more pain medications helped.

Our midwife simply kept saying that it was all normal to feel like I did because it was part of 'natural' childbirth. She solely focused on other things like teaching us how to give Elsie her first bath or how to wrap her tightly in a muslin cloth to help her sleep. As I mentioned, our main midwife was part of a team, and another midwife from the team also visited the house, on the days our main midwife was off or at another birth. The second midwife was different from the first. They each had different ideas about certain things, and each gave us conflicting advice on so many aspects, including breastfeeding and co-sleeping. It was very confusing. We felt stuck, trying to find out information on Google and also accept the different advice coming from family members – it was all so conflicting and confusing. We didn't know who to trust in the end – let alone ourselves. The most frustrating part was when people said to just 'trust your own motherly instincts'. I was trying to, but the 'instincts' I was having about my pain and not feeling right were only ever met with 'you're fine, it's all normal', so my ability to judge situations and act on 'motherly instinct' was skewed.

Help me!

The pain wasn't improving downstairs and I felt 'off'. I was so very petrified of looking down there, that I just didn't. However, within the first week or so, and with the pain getting worse, not better, I decided it was time to see what was going on. A pungent smell was coming from down there, too. I still couldn't sit down and certainly was in no position to bend over to see what was going on, so I took a photo.

What I saw on that screen looking back at me was mortifying. I now knew why I didn't want to look in the first place. My entire groin was black, blue and purple. Beyond the bruising, I actually didn't know what I was looking at. What is that? I could see a big, gaping wound, opened up with raw flesh exposed. It was hard to tell what was what. I actually couldn't tell what part was my vulva and what part was the wound. I did understand what the smell was, however: infection where my stitching had come undone. It was just such a mess.

Standing half-dressed in the bathroom, I yelled out to Tom to call our midwife straightaway. He got her on the phone and started asking me questions through the door and relaying the information back to her. She told him that it sounded normal. I felt anything but normal. It took some more back and forth through the door before she said that if I was really worried, I should pop down to our GP. So I did.

Our GP was also a great listener. He fitted me into his already busy afternoon schedule but, when I arrived, he explained that unfortunately he was not able to have a look to see what was going on that day because no female nurse (or doctor) was available to assist with the appointment. This was policy at this practice (which I had no clue about until in this moment of need). I cried, thinking

I was not going to get the help I needed. We talked in more detail about what was happening down there and he agreed to start me on antibiotics with a follow-up appointment booked for the next day (with the female nurse assisting).

The next morning, Tom took me and Elsie back to the GP's surgery. Everyone was gushing over our little baby girl – not nearly as much as we were. Lying back on the bed I watched two professionals' faces change from 'baby gush' to 'shock and OMG'. Then my GP said, 'Oh, darling, what happened to you? There is a lot going on there.'

My stitching was all coming undone. It certainly was infected. No wonder I could not sit down. The wound was tearing along the right side of my butt, along the sit bone. My GP gave me a second prescription for much stronger antibiotics. I needed to take both types to try to get rid of this infection. All the while, I was more worried about Elsie and how the antibiotics could affect her through the breast milk. I timed taking the meds around her feeds to be on the safer side. My GP also said to have a salt bath.

The next day, it was our alternate midwife's turn to do the home visit. I told her about the wound and visiting the GP. She had a quick look and then decided to show me how to breastfeed laying on my side. That was really hard. It was obviously less painful than trying to sit on my butt, but much harder for Elsie because of the logistics. Being in so much pain and not being able to get it right with Elsie all became overwhelming. There were a lot of tears and not just from the newborn.

No visitors please, something's not right

Later that night, I still felt off. We hadn't allowed too many visitors because I wanted to be better before having everyone visit. Close immediate family and my bestie, Sharn, were the exception. Sharn and her hubby both had medical backgrounds, and I turned to them for advice every day. Her hubby would pop in on the way home from work to check on us. I remember that night after the midwife's visit clearly. I was trying to breastfeed lying down as the midwife had showed me that afternoon. As he walked in the room, I started crying. And then I cried some more. And cried some more. I was in so much pain, both downstairs and in my heart.

We planned for Sharn and her hubby to have a long visit the following day. I knew it would cheer me up to see Sharn, and it did. Our midwife came for a flying visit in the morning and I told her how I was feeling – crying a lot and feeling off. 'Yep, all normal Steph.'

Sharn and hubby came for afternoon tea. As they walked into our lounge room they both looked at me a little strangely. I thought something was wrong with them. They looked at each other, and then back at me. Then Sharn asked me if I was feeling okay. I said, 'The same as yesterday and the day before that.' Her hubby quickly went to his car to grab some stuff.

He came back with a blood pressure cuff and told me to lie down. The look he gave his wife before talking to me scared me. He told me not to move. The reading was very low – under 80/60. I was not well. My skin was pale and my pulse weak. I finally felt like someone was listening to me when I said I wasn't feeling 'normal' (not even the 'I just had a baby' kind of normal).

Time to talk: the 'normal' story just doesn't match what's happening

During our midwife's next visit, I really wanted to talk to her about a few things. My mum had been asking so many questions about the birth, ones I was not able to answer. I had been giving Mum the brush off, telling her 'it was all normal, Mum' (just like our midwife had been telling us). But the 'normal' story was wearing thin for us all.

I'd decided to wait for the next visit, rather than call my midwife. And I certainly couldn't text her. The midwife-led program had certain rules after birth too, and this was one of them. You were only allowed to call your midwife, not text. So it was confusing when they would text me about certain things and I would try to reply (to their text) with a text and be told not to do that. I went along with it, of course. I was still trying to be the good patient.

It so happened that the morning our midwife arrived, my mum was visiting too. It was all pleasantries at first. As she was doing all the checks on Elsie, I started asking some of the questions Mum wanted to know the answers for, the ones she kept pushing me on. What had happened to Elsie's scalp, for example, and what happened during the birth.

Our midwife started with her famous four words: 'It was all normal'. She did say the second stage went a 'little longer' and that I was fatigued. She didn't provide a lot of detail, actually. She did say that my episiotomy was probably a little bigger than it needed to be.

Once she had finished the weighing and measuring and was packing up, she dropped a bomb. Today was going to be her last visit. *What?* It was only the seventh or eighth visit, and the program was meant to run for ten visits after coming home. I was surprised and scared at the same time. So surprised and scared that all I could manage to say was, 'I wish I would have known, because I wanted to buy you a thank-you gift.'

What I really wanted to say was, 'What do we do now?' So many things were still happening, for me and Elsie.

And what? It gets worse?

I had no idea the worst was yet to come.

The swelling had subsided a little with each day. I was checking on the wound periodically. Apart from the reduced swelling, it was the same. Still open. Still sore to sit on. At about day ten, after the shower I took a quick snap and what looked back at me from the screen had me in a panic. Was that another baby's head crowning? Was I having twins and no-one knew? Did they leave one in there?

As irrational as these ideas and fears seem now, at the time they were real (sleep deprivation wouldn't have helped). It certainly looked like a baby head was crowning from my vagina. Something

After birth

round and pink was popping out. It was 7 pm and we didn't know what to do. So we did the only thing we knew and phoned our midwife. Again Tom and I were talking through the door. Tom was on the phone with the midwife and I was holding this photo, trying to describe what it was (there was no way in the world I was going to show him). As soon as I heard her pull out the 'it's all fine and normal' line, I screamed at the top of my lungs, 'IT'S NOT FUCKING FINE, I'M NOT FUCKING FINE'.

Leaning over the bathroom basin, crying uncontrollably by this stage, I'd had enough of being told that I was normal – and fine. Clearly my broken vagina was not normal or fine. It was time to take matters into our own hands. Our midwife was not providing any help and certainly no support. Her last day had come and gone. She was gone.

After hanging up from the midwife, I frantically called Sharn and her hubby to ask their medical opinion of the symptoms. They told me I should go back to hospital to be checked, but that it probably wasn't a matter of urgency. It was so late at night by this stage, Elsie was crying, I was crying. We decided that the emergency department was no place for a newborn baby and that we would get on to it first thing in the morning – plus the people we needed to see probably wouldn't be there until 'office hours' anyway.

I was on the phone first thing the next morning with my GP and the hospital where I'd given birth to try to get some help. I demanded that someone at the hospital see me. I wanted to see an obstetrician or doctor this time. I had many conversations, repeating my symptoms to the reception nurse, her supervisor and then their supervisor, but all to no avail. I then went through my calendar to look for the name of the obstetrician we met once during the early days, the one who helped me during the difficult time with boss man at work. I found the appointment and worked out his name was Simon Winder. I phoned the hospital again and asked for him directly. I lied and said I was his current patient. At the time he was busy and had to call me back. When he did call me back - finally – I was listened to and we had an appointment to meet him during his lunchtime that same day. He listened to every word I was saying before examining the wound. With authority, he told me to stop salt baths and that I would possibly require repair surgery under general aesthetic (which scared me because it would interrupt breastfeeding), but he wanted to give it another day or two, trying a different antibiotic and treatment plan (which ultimately worked). He explained the answers to all our questions about the gaping wound but he didn't go into a lot of detail about anything else (possibly because everything was still too swollen). He too said 'this' can happen after childbirth and gave me a referral for the physiotherapy department at the hospital. We walked from his appointment straight up to the physiotherapy department to make the appointment to fix 'this'. Even with the four to five week wait, I made an appointment, not knowing what 'this' really was or what it meant at the time. We were still in the dark.

Once home, this round, pink, head-shaped thing hanging out of my vagina was freaking me out. I could hardly walk. It was heavy. It was uncomfortable to stand or sit by this stage. I was petrified it would fall out, along with all of my insides, right into the toilet or my undies. I didn't really share these feelings about 'this' with anyone because I was worried about the judgement about being a big 'worrier', and a paranoid new mum with too much anxiety about everything.

Google to the rescue ...

Google can be your worst enemy, but it can also be helpful when looking for people and services. Through Google, I discovered a private women's physio just around the corner from our place. I quickly rang them and begged for (and got) an appointment with Kate. She was lovely, and she knew her stuff. She was not able to do an internal examination because it was too soon post-partum, but was able to look at the round pink thing and tell me she suspected it was a prolapse.

A what? Pro-what? 'What the prolapse' does this mean?

I fired so many questions at Kate. She warned me repeatedly that it was too soon to officially diagnose, but then told me it was possibly my bladder falling down in the vaginal wall and through the opening of my vagina. I think she did try to reassure me that it would not detach and completely fall out, like I had imagined. This all happened as Elsie was lying on a beautiful knitted blanket on the floor beside me. I kept looking to my beautiful newborn baby, perhaps for some reassurance. I don't know. I think I was in shock and denial that this was happening. That it was now a real thing. Another thing to try to deal with on top of attempting the hardest job in the world, being a new parent.

Our experience of struggling through the next few weeks was probably similar to that of most new parents trying to find their feet. We were tired but still tried to focus on those moments of joy, and our love for our new baby. At the same time, it was shit-hard for me to pretend that it was all okay. We told no-one what was happening, partly because it was not officially confirmed but also because it was not part of that baby woowoo everyone wants to see and talk about. People don't really want to know that it feels like your bladder is hanging out of your vagina.

I did attend all of the appointments with the hospital physiotherapist as well as those with Kate. I wanted to make sure I covered all bases. They both gave me homework to do (lots of pelvic floor exercises). Kate even showed me a device that looked a lot like a vibrator – only no fun. This one gave little electric shocks to the pelvic floor muscles to try to strengthen them. This broken vagina needed to be fixed so I could get on with being a new mumma.

The hospital visits were all very positive, with lots of positive talk about how well I was doing. I was on the right track, I was told. It was hard work, but I never missed a day of doing what was asked of me from both physios. It just didn't seem to be making much difference. My prolapse still hung out. It was still painful to walk or stand.

In the end, I only stayed working with Kate. The hospital became dismissive when I said that I didn't feel any better and they only allow for a few visits post birth. I left my last hospital appointment with a flier for a pessary (a device you insert into the vagina to prevent the 'protrusion of pelvic structures' – in my case, to stop my bladder coming out). I showed Kate the flyer and she explained to me the different pessary types and sizes. I remember being horrified at one ring she showed me, and thinking – is that for a human or a cow? How can something that large even fit in through the opening of the vagina (which is ridiculous as they stretch much more than a pessary during labour). Kate was both methodical and knowledgeable and spoke of her own personal experience. She used instruments to measure before and then again after treatments. She also attempted to fit me with a pessary, testing a few different ones at different stages. I threw everything I could at this prolapse and even signed up for special pelvic floor physio classes, three times a week. I spent a good seven months doing all the therapy and classes. At the end of each day, I would feed Elsie, then pump (trying to keep up breastfeeding), and then stick the electronic stimulator into my vagina for half an hour before falling into bed. I'm sure Tom was there too, but we never seemed to 'see' each other during those nights.

My gut feeling was right, however. All the pelvic floor exercises and electric shocks under the sun were not making an inch of difference.

Post the postpartum and still no better

Once we had worked out through Kate's clinical assessment and measurements that things were not making a difference, my big question was where I should go from here. Kate suggested a few things, and I did all of them. I made an appointment with the pelvic floor unit at St George Hospital in Sydney. At the same time, I tried to book another appointment with Dr Simon Winder, but I was told he had since resigned from the hospital and I couldn't find him anywhere on Google. I was then referred to another local private obstetrician, Dr Greening.

Tom and I went to see Dr Greening together, and it turned out Tom and Dr Greening were cycling 'in the same circles'. They spoke a lot about riding, until it was time to get down to business. Back in the consult room after an internal examination in both vagina and anus (which I was not expecting), he broke the news, telling me 'it was like an abyss'. He went on to explain that the pelvic floor muscle didn't feel attached. This was not part of his normal obstetrics duties so he sent us to see a private laparoscopic surgeon in Sydney.

Because Elsie hated car rides so much, I did this one on my own. This surgeon was a softly spoken man who had a kind demeanour about him. He, too, did an internal examination and echoed what Dr Greening had said. Only this time, his diagnosis was worse. The surgery he would normally offer to repair this kind of damage was not going to be suitable because it just would not hold and I would have to go through the whole trauma again. Meaning, it was not able to be fixed. At the time I thought, *Great, if you can't do it laparoscopically, then someone else can – surely.*

He then gave me the sucker punch blow… no more babies.

This was something I certainly was not expecting. Dr Greening had spoken to me about possibly needing a C-section next time. But this! Having more babies was not part of our daily conversations at home at that very moment. We were too focused on getting fixed and just surviving first. They were always in the plan, though. (Remember me wanting six babies? Well, I think we'd settled on two or three.)

This surgeon explained that it would not be a good idea seeing as I was having so many issues just trying to care for Elsie as it was. This somewhat made sense. I just didn't want it to be the case. I just didn't want to hear that. I left that appointment with a heavy heart. Some hard conversations would need to be had at home. The emotional roller-coaster continued (and I go into this in more detail in the next chapter).

Elsie was getting to an age where she was able to move around and do more things on her own. We loved watching every minute. At the same time I did feel ripped off that I had missed so much because of this prolapse. Tom and I felt so lucky and blessed that Elsie had come into our world, and we no longer felt like there was something missing for us. We were fulfilled. Maybe one child was perfect for us. That saying 'one and done' made total sense to us at this point. Then the conversation took an unexpected turn. What about Elsie? What about her needs? Would she be happiest being an only child or would she like to have a buddy, a little sibling? Tom and I both had older siblings. Our parents all had siblings. What were we to do?

Exploring second (and third and fourth) opinions

First things first: we need to make sure what this surgeon had told us was set in stone. Perhaps someone else could fix the prolapse so we could have more children. We needed to be sure, so went to our appointment with the pelvic floor unit at St George hospital with the aim of having an answer by the end of the appointment.

The appointment itself was let-down after let-down. When I originally phoned to make the appointment, I explained my situation and was told that they could do a 3D scan to see exactly what was going on in there. I knew we were on the right track because this was something Kate suggested that might be needed.

This time we paid someone to care for Elsie because this was a very important appointment for us and Tom needed to be there. We arrived only to be told that the guy who could provide the scan was on long-service leave. That's okay, we said, someone else can do it, right? Nope, just that one guy. We felt so frustrated after going to all this effort just to be here. I was able to move past that, however, knowing that the specialist we wanted to talk to about getting pregnant again was there, and she had a great reputation.

We were shown into the consult room and at first spoke with a registrar. I had to go through the whole story again, but thought it was just part of the process before the actual specialist came in. After speaking with the registrar, I was seen by a nurse to have a different pessary fitted. I got to take this one for a 'test run' – literally. She helped to insert it and asked me to go outside for a run. I did. For the first two minutes it was okay, and definitely felt better than having the bladder hang out.

Then flop! It fell out into my undies along with the bladder. Dishevelled, I waddled like a duck back inside and told her it was no good. This process continued until one seemed to be the better fit and stayed in. Sold! It was mine to take home. The nurse then went to show us out. 'Hang on,' we said. 'What about talking with the specialist about another baby?' The nurse left the room to go and get her, and we thought there must simply have been a communication error or something.

Nope. The registrar came back and said the appointment was finished. I stressed that we had come a long way and we really just wanted ten minutes of the specialist's time. We were told she was 'too busy' to see us. She passed on the message that we were fine to have another baby. While this was what I wanted to hear, I needed to hear it with a little more conviction than a second-hand (and seemingly pretty flippant) comment. Adding insult to injury, as we were walking out we saw the specialist sitting at the tea table enjoying a nice cuppa. 'Too busy'?! Oh, and halfway back to the car the second pessary flopped out. We couldn't go back for another fitting with no-one available to see us, and our babysitter's time was up and we needed to get back. Awesome! That was a complete waste of time.

I sat silent most of the two-hour car ride home. Tom knew that couldn't be good. I now had a new mission ...

Ask yourself ...

- Have you ever been told (perhaps repeatedly) that something was normal and at first accepted this advice because it came from someone you trusted? What was your gut telling you?

- What is your experience with seeing specialists (if any)? Did they give you the attention and time you needed, or did you leave with unanswered questions? How did the specialist make you feel?

CHAPTER 5
AFTER THE AFTER BIRTH

*D*riving home from the St George pelvic floor unit, I felt like I was stuck in limbo land, between two very opposing opinions – one saying 'no more babies' and the other a somewhat casual 'sure, go ahead, have another baby'. There was no way I was going to just let it be like this forever. We had to make a decision, and that decision had to be well-thought out. To be able to even get there, however, we needed all the information we could find – and so to reading through online forums, and checking Google and Facebook pages. Finding information on pelvic floor issues and pregnancy wasn't easy – unlike finding all the woowoo info about how lovely everything about natural childbirth and pregnancy is. For this info, I had to dig deeper.

Each night, we would put Elsie to bed and, instead of resting or spending precious time with my husband, I would sit on the internet for hours, looking for ways to get help, ways to be fixed. Then I found him: Professor Hans Peter Dietz. He had written an article about pelvic floor injury caused by vaginal births, and everything he described in the article rang true. He talked about the symptoms and lack of information, and it was like he was talking specifically about me. I needed to talk with this guy. From the last experience at the pelvic floor unit, however, I didn't have too much hope about getting in touch with him, let alone him seeing me.

Well, that was anything but the truth. I flicked off an email and within a day or two he arranged a chat over the phone. This call went for well over an hour. He knew so much, and it was so reassuring to hear that how I felt about what I was going through was not all in my head. It was not normal to have these injuries. Oh, and he also did the 3D/4D scans.

Meeting Professor Dietz was amazing. Like Kate, he was methodical. Things were measured and examinations performed thoroughly. (He didn't just shove his hand inside me to feel around.) This appointment was long – a few hours all up – with lots of testing by his assistants and, when they had finished, lots of talking. Professor Dietz talks fast and there was a lot to be said, so the exact order of words is hard to remember verbatim. Importantly, though, he spoke with conviction and we had confidence in what he was saying. He talked about the extent of the damage in medical terminology and that a surgery option might be possible. This full surgery would be unlike the laparoscopic (or keyhole) surgery one discussed with the surgeon. Professor Dietz's one caveat on surgery was that we needed to be finished having babies.

What? We can have another baby? 'Yes, of course you can, Stephanie.' Professor Dietz explained all the damage had been done already, and another baby wouldn't cause more damage. 'You just won't let anyone use forceps on you again,' he told me. I kind of flicked my head to the side and pursed my lips for a moment, wondering what he meant by that. I had a million questions running through my mind at that moment, including *How will I be able to carry another baby?* but couldn't form the words to say anything. It was Tom who spoke up and asked, 'Why no forceps?' This opened a 'Pandora's box' for Professor Dietz, and he went on to provide great detail and all the medical stats as to why forceps should not be used and why the resulting damage to my pelvic floor was totally preventable. The passion in his voice was clear: he was not a fan of forceps.

This was not the last we spoke of pregnancy and childbirth. In fact, I think I had him on speed dial with all my questions about carrying another baby – all of which he answered, every time.

What a relief. We left that appointment on cloud nine, and had a very different car ride home. We chatted all the way home about more babies. Elsie wasn't even one yet. While we did think it was a bit too soon, in the back of our minds we also didn't want to wait another five years before being able to fall pregnant, like the first time. I now also had an end goal, to have babies and then get fixed – so I could be that mum I wanted to be.

Decision time

After lots more discussion, Tom and I made a decision. It was a hard one to make, but we decided if I wasn't pregnant by the end of the year (which was only three months away), we were going to call it. Elsie was going to be our one and only. Having the surgery was so important to me. I was missing so much and wanted to be normal again.

IVF was certainly off the table – our home already had enough going on in it. We did have to figure out a way to even get pregnant. Yes, we know 'how' it normally works. It was just going to be harder this time. Things were not normal for me down there. I wanted to be pregnant and have another baby. It was the actual first part of the process of baby-making that I was scared of most. Sex is possible (with planning, including getting the time of day right), but sex and intimacy have never been the same.

The emotional roller-coaster of fear, pain, hurting and anger I was on, cycled through on a daily basis. When we received good news (like finding out we were even able to have another baby), we were on a high. Every time we hit a stumbling block, however, I hit rock bottom. The physical side of things was hard. Tom was really the only person I told. I'm sure at some point he started to become numb to the daily 'pain conversations'.

This was hard for us, and hard for our marriage. We put brave faces on each day, for one another and the outside world. The woowoo of a new baby was all about big smiles, laughing and gushing over our baby girl. We certainly did have those feelings too, but at the same time we were both suffering in silence.

We pushed down our pain and suffering. It was much easier to pretend than to try to explain what we ourselves didn't really understand.

We were the 'happy little family'.

Ask yourself ...

- How good are you at talking about your feelings when you are in pain or suffering? How does this change when the pain and suffering is ongoing?

- How often have you felt you just need to 'soldier on' rather than talk through problems or get help?

CHAPTER 6
THE (UN)HAPPY LITTLE FAMILY

*L*et me start this chapter by saying we are a typical nuclear family: two parents with kids. Throughout this chapter, I refer to the 'husband' and 'wife', because this is true to our story. However, all of the following information applies to any family with partnered parents. I know I'm not the ABC (which as Australia's national broadcaster is expected to always be completely balanced), but inclusivity is so important when talking about making way for change in this space.

Returning to our journey, Elsie was turning one. We could hardly believe it. A part of me didn't want to believe it. I liked to still say her age in months rather than simply one year. She still sounded more like a baby that way.

But she was turning one, so let the celebrations begin! And we went BIG. We combined her birthday with her naming day. It was unlike me to want big. Our wedding was lovely and intimate, relaxed and fun. But this was a mega celebration because we didn't think it would happen again – that is, celebrating another baby's first birthday. We hired a huge house, a local caterer and a jumping castle. Parts of my wedding dress were used to make her naming-day gown. We had special candles made for her godparents, grandparents and special guests. Tom and I even splurged on new outfits.

It was an amazing day and weekend. Family and friends gathered under a beautiful big tree as our marriage celebrant blessed Elsie on her naming day. We were so lucky to have everyone there to help celebrate with us. Tom surprised me with an eternity ring, and presented it to me in front of everyone. It was all very unlike him, and very unlike me. I loved his speech to me. He thanked me for everything I was doing every day for Elsie, which everyone thought was lovely. Only he and I really knew the impact of that thank you and ring. Our silent struggle was still silent.

So what about the dad?

Tom is a truly amazing man. He is kind and so loving. His level of support throughout this journey has been indescribable. We both ride the roller-coaster of emotions and, more times than not, can help the other one if they're stuck on the bottom. And try to work it so we're both on the top. We work well together. Always have.

I'm sure this has come at a cost to him somewhere along the way, even if he doesn't show it. I'm sure it has. He, too, lost his wife that day. The normal we all longed for was gone for him as well. He never complains when I have a 'bad day' and can't move or function. He simply picks up where I left off – be that cooking dinner, caring for our kids or sending me to get a massage – he always thinks of my needs. Many times, my self-doubt has taken me to scary places about our relationship. I have wondered what his thoughts about our birthing suite experience might really be. The 'real' ones. The ones he won't ever share with me, to protect me.

He has now seen me at my most vulnerable. I no longer have my (post-cancer) 'tough cookie' face on when we are alone. My insecurities have taunted me along the lines of, 'We will never be the same, and yet he still stays'. I have this silly car analogy (because Tom loves cars so much). I used to feel like Tom had his Ferrari wife, something he worked hard to achieve in his life. He loved it so much, cared for it, cherished it and loved people to know how proud he was of it. And then, in an instant, one day he woke up and it was gone. No more Ferrari. It had been taken away, never to be found. All he was left with was a shitty, falling to bits, rusty old Datsun. And even if he misses his Ferrari, and yearns for it, he just has to be grateful for still having some mode of transport. (At times I think he might feel he has no choice.)

It has taken a long time for me to see my actual worth. Some days I'm better at believing it than others. Most days, I know I'm simply doing everything I can, the best I can. Don't get me wrong – there have been some bullshit hard times. When pain and emotions run high, it gets tough. It has taken three years of us working through things to be where we are today. He continues to grow with me and ride that roller-coaster – and know that the downs don't always last too long.

We have learnt one great tip along the way: don't take it week by week, or even day by day. When shit gets real and nothing is working (physically, mentally or emotionally), just take it hour by hour (or even in blocks of minutes when it's really tough). If it's 11.34 am and you still haven't showered, the baby is crying, you've got no money in the bank, you need to do the shopping but you are in pain, take 10 minutes, take the hour to reset. Even if the next hour looks much the same, a point will come in the day where that will change. Trust the process. We have learnt this one the hard way.

I have been to see a number of counsellors post birth. Some were good, while some were not so good. The one I've been working with the longest is wonderful. She works with many mummas like me, and I have learnt so much about myself during this process. Initially I wanted her to 'fix' me. I soon learnt that it does not work that way.

Tom deals with things by exercising or working stupidly hard and I worried about how this birth had affected him. We have only spoken about it a few times but, from what he has shared with me, he feels like he let me down. He didn't know what was going on. He had no clue what to do when it all went south. He felt helpless.

It certainly didn't help that my mum wasn't able to show him any empathy, saying things like, 'I'll be there next time to make sure this doesn't happen again'. Cut me to the core that one. Of course, because he is the way he is, Tom didn't say anything, but it was written all over his face. Even if I didn't believe any of that to be true, at all! He heard his own insecurities being said back by someone else, so he thought it must have been true.

In the birthing classes, Tom was only ever taught how to be that happy cheerleader, and how to stroke my back during the 'surges'. He was never told about what to do when his wife looks desperately at him for the right answers when facing big decisions at the 11th hour (or, in our case, the 25th hour) of birth. There certainly was no talk about how to look for signs of post-natal depression, PTSD or even how to help your wife when she doesn't even know what is going on.

I can only imagine that we not alone here. Helping dads and partners understand and be more educated would be one of the 'easier' places to start in making way for change. Helping everyone understand would hopefully take some of the pressure away from the mummas, and help them stop feeling like they're responsible to know everything. Two parents, making informed decisions together, seems a good outcome for everyone. And in some circles, I'm sure it already has started.

Tom and I have had to navigate our way through some tricky times when it comes to trying our best to be a 'normal' family. What was normal three years ago looks very different to our normal now. Letting go of ideals and goals held for most of our lives has been difficult and it hurts.

Part of the quest to be normal was to give Elsie a sibling. It was for her. The discussions with a number of professionals had already happened and we were able to make our own decision, knowing as much as we could. It took Elsie's month of birthday celebrations for me to be relaxed enough to even consider trying to make a baby. I was so intensely stressed about being intimate with my husband again that it took me a few wines to think it was even physically possible.

From three to four

As you can imagine, after all those years of trying to fall pregnant with Elsie, we were totally shocked to discover we were now pregnant with baby two. And it happened so quickly, well within the three-month deadline we'd given ourselves. My thoughts relentlessly flickered between happiness and fear. This birth needed to be in total opposition to the first, and I certainly had moments of thinking that I couldn't do this.

We very quickly became caught up in all the woowoo. How lovely for Elsie to be a big sissy. This was great. Well, at least that was what we kept telling ourselves.

It was getting close to Christmas and I was due to see Professor Dietz again to plan for surgery the following year. I was still keeping my eye on the prize with the end goal of being 'fixed'. The conversation stopped once we shared that we were expecting another baby in the middle of the following year. He said to call him again once baby had arrived and we were certain there would be no more babies. I had so many more questions for him about this pregnancy and birth, which we had been working through over the phone. At our last appointment, he told me that the pregnancy would actually help the prolapse symptoms. And he was right – as my uterus grew outwards, it 'lifted' everything upward, making it less noticeable. I still wanted to know how the hell I was going to get this baby out, however. I thought the only way was to have a caesarean (surely).

No. He had a very different idea. He repeated what he'd told me earlier, saying something like, 'Sorry to say, all the damage has already been done' and that there should be nothing stopping me trying to birth vaginally, as long as there was no use of forceps.

(I loved that he never used the words 'naturally' or 'normal', because this took the pressure off.)

From that moment, I knew I needed more autonomy and guidance through this next birth. It was time to find us an obstetrician, and I remembered Dr Simon Winder. Tom and I both liked him, and his kind bedside manner and calmness. I searched high and low for him and finally tracked him down at a newly opened private hospital, where the reception staff said he was setting up rooms, but that they didn't have a start date or way to contact him. I phoned the main hospital switchboard so many times looking for him, they let me leave my number for him to call me.

When that call didn't come, I asked my GP for other suggestions. He referred us to one of the oldest OBs in town. I guess he thought he would have the most experience, and he might have, but possibly the least amount of good bedside manner. After our first appointment, we thought maybe he'd been in the game too long. His words to us were pretty much, 'You're only seven weeks. Let's just see if it lasts first.' What the fuck?! Who says that to parents who have just poured their hearts out about their struggles to fall pregnant and then the trauma of the first birth? We had no faith in him being able to provide the level of care we needed for this next birth, so back to the drawing board we went.

I kept phoning the private hospital to track down Simon. One day I was chatting with friends when the call came. It was him! Simon did phone me back. We spoke for an hour on the phone before making the first appointment, and that first appointment went for over two hours. It was more like a counselling session for me and Tom, and we had a lot to say. Simon was great, and so understanding. And even though he had ended up resigning from the public hospital soon after Elsie's birth, in protest to what was happening there (to lots of mummas), he still maintained a level of professionalism during all our discussions.

Happy little family

We were on the right track to that normal, 'happy little family'. Yay!

This time we shared the news earlier with our family than the 12-week 'silence code' allowed. It was Christmas and I wasn't drinking, so my cousins would've soon worked it out anyway. I also had all those same fuzzy, buzzy feelings downstairs, just like with Elsie. I didn't listen to old obstetrician guy. This baby was making its way to us.

And this time I was on even more of a fact-finding mission. Instead of looking at woowoo pics on Instagram, or only buying the books with similar images on the front cover, I focused on medical journals and academic books. The problem was not much was out there. The lack of public information about how to birth after birth trauma was practically non-existent.

So for the next seven months until the birth, I spoke with as many people as I could – doctors, midwives, doulas and mummas. I hounded Simon and Prof Dietz with every worry. It was much better to feel like I was a little annoying than feel like I was just putting my head in the sand. This baby was coming out one way or another and I needed to be better equipped this time. The pregnancy went well, with no gestational diabetes this time, which was surprising. (I had thought once you had it for your first birth, you would always get it.) And I found it reassuring that maybe this baby wouldn't be as big.

The fear of not being able to carry to full term also came into my head. As I've mentioned, my fear that the prolapse would get worse during pregnancy turned out to be unfounded. During the second trimester, the prolapse actually felt somewhat less bothersome. It was great, so normal. By the third trimester, it did start to sag back down (to where it was before), but because I was distracted with being pregnant and all the uncomfortable joys it brings, I didn't really notice a huge difference. It also helped that I was so busy and distracted with Elsie running around now.

The mental stuff about the birth, on the other hand, was thick. The anxiety and worry about how I was possibly going to birth this little baby was playing on my mind the closer I got to my due date. In my visual thoughts, I could see the bladder blocking the opening of the vagina and the baby trying to push its way out. I thought of the bladder like a plug. How the hell was baby going to get past that? Would my organs all fall out onto the delivery bed? I (clearly) needed a C-section.

Dr Winder and I spoke at length about this very thing – a lot, at every appointment. I actually had no real idea what a C-section was before these discussions. I knew your tummy was cut open and that you couldn't drive for a few weeks afterwards, but that was about it. So I asked him to step me through the whole process involved in a C-section. I wanted to know every single detail and every single risk. The more I heard, the more I realised this wasn't as easy as others had made out. At each appointment, I would ask him my new list of questions. I'm sure they were really the same thing, just asked in a different way. Will this work? Will it break me again? Will I (mentally) survive if there was more trauma?

Through all these discussions with Dr Winder and Professor Dietz, we developed a plan A and a plan B, and then a backup plan too. We talked about specifics – such as using a catheter to ensure my bladder was empty and birthing lying on my side to ensure my bladder was in the optimal position. Taking in the advice given by both my trusted professionals, we decided that because a vaginal birth was in fact possible, I would attempt it. I was okay with this advice in my head and yet my heart was taking a while to be convinced I could go through this again. Hence, the plan was to keep the communication channels open prior and during the birth and, if at any stage I was not mentally okay, a planned caesarean could be performed. The other plan was, of course, if at any stage it looked like I needed some medical help, a caesarean would be performed over the use of vacuum or forceps. Simon was there to support my own decisions the entire way.

All this ended up meaning I was a lot more comfortable leading up to the birth this time round. I felt more informed and so did Tom. Well, really, we knew that we didn't want a repeat of the trauma in the first and ran towards what we did want.

Plan B already?!

A few weeks out from the due date, I met with Simon and had another great appointment. Each ultrasound he would sometimes forget if we wanted to know the sex of our baby and ask me, 'You know what you're having, right?' And I would say, 'Yep, a baby.' It was great we could laugh and joke like that. Then he would always say, 'Great, because it's very obvious.' As I was leaving this appointment, however, things went a little differently. Simon walked me out to the reception area, where the next pregnant couple were already waiting. (I'm sure we always went over time because of all my questions.) We said our goodbyes and I said, 'See you next week'. And then he dropped his bombshell. 'Oh, hang on. I'm just popping over to the states for a few days, so we'll need to make your next appointment a few days later than normal.'

'What did you just say?' I said. 'The states, as in United States of America?!! Like the one that is 20 hours away?' I laughed as I said this, thinking (hoping) I'd heard it wrong or he was kind of joking. He was not smiling now.

'Yes, Steph, the USA. But it's only for a few days and I'll be back.'

I put my brave face on and nodded, silently. Trying to convince myself that, so close to my due date, it was okay the ONLY person I trusted in this world to deliver my baby was not going to be in the country for a few days. He ushered the next appointment through. I paid the lovely reception lady and slid on out the door, probably only making it ten steps or so before starting to shake. My knees were weak. I was having 'a moment' – beyond the normal pregnant, hormonal kind. It was more like the ones you see on TV, when the young girl gets her heart broken for the first time.

My back slammed against the wall and I slid down to the floor. I was uncontrollably crying. My heart WAS breaking – literally.

What if this baby decided to come early? I could not do this without Simon. I don't know how long I sat on the floor crying. I could not move. The pain and hurt in my heart was so intense. And partly too because my belly was so big at that stage I had to commando-roll to get myself off the floor. I had to pick up Elsie, so on went the sunnies and into the lift I went to get out of the building (like sunnies would hide the tears). The sadness and fear hung around like a bad smell. Nothing could really distract me from worrying about what would happen if bub arrived while Simon was gone. I had to clear my head. This worry was not healthy. So I wrote Simon an email, telling him all the things I was worried about. Even if I didn't send it, at least writing it down meant it was out of my head.

In the end, I did send it, and Simon called me back. He apologised that he'd left me feeling that way. We talked at great length. He was confident baby was not going to come that early. But if that was to happen, we did have a plan B. So Tom and I met with his obstetrician colleague, who was also a nice guy and good listener, and also showed compassion and seemed to understand our history. He was not Simon, though.

If I could have turned myself upside down for that week, I would have. I would have done anything to stop baby from wanting to arrive. We even visited our local Buddhist temple. I prayed to everyone and anyone. Baby had to wait – and, happily, baby did wait. Back in Simon's office the following week, we could all have a 'little' laugh about it. Phew. I was now ready when baby was ready.

See you next Tuesday!

After our little laugh, Simon jumped in with, 'So when do you want to have this baby?' Like it was now a choice. I was confused. Didn't baby say when it was ready, like last time? This time was different and this choice was different. We talked at length about an induction due to my high level of anxiety and fear of the unknown again. I needed to be able to have more autonomy. I know you cannot always control all aspects of childbirth but I did want to minimise any level of trauma. At this stage, we were still talking about vaginal birth and caesarean birth, even though an overall plan A had been decided on. My head was still thinking I could not push baby out. But I did make a choice on the birth date.

'Next Tuesday it is then. See you next week.' *Yay!* I thought. And, of course, the decision-making process was more detailed than simply placing my finger on any random date on the calendar. I was already showing early signs of labour, including losing the mucus plug and baby's head was engaged. We spoke at length again about the baby, its needs along with mine and when it was going to be ready.

When I told Tom, he had the same face as I imagine I did when Simon asked me which day would work. *Really, just like that?* 'Yep,' I said. 'We are going to meet our little baby boy next Tuesday.' We shifted from fear to excitement now.

Spending the last weekend with Elsie as our only child is something I will never forget. We made it count. That Sunday afternoon, the sun was out. We took her to the beach for a walk with my family, and shared some very special times. Tom took lots of photos and captured the most precious video. I was sitting on a park bench with my sister and Elsie came running towards me calling, 'Mumma, mumma'. We embraced. We both held on tight.

On the Monday night as I put Elsie to bed, I teared up a little. I was sad to be away from her the next day – and the following few days while birthing her sibling. I was going to miss her. I already missed her. I had to keep telling myself that it was okay, because this was FOR her. Then early Tuesday morning quickly came around. My mum and dad were there to take care of Elsie. The bags were packed and we said our goodbyes to my parents before she woke up.

The roads were still quiet. It was winter and the air was cold and frosty and the windows had condensation on them. Tom drove ever so slowly, like we already had our newborn baby son in the back. We were greeted with a big smile from the nurse in the maternity floor, and she showed us to the delivery suites. We felt a few nerves, but overall we were feeling okay. Once we entered the room, our excitement went to the next level. This time we were in a private hospital. (We'd updated our private health insurance after Elsie's birth, even though at the time we were not sure about being able to have another baby. All bases had to be covered just in case. No way in hell was I ever stepping foot in that other hospital again.) The room was made up just for us, and it had a warm feeling about it. Everything was laid out on the bed. I remember feeling special that baby's ID bracelet was already waiting on the warmed baby cot, next to the little singlet and nappy they provided.

We met our midwife and did the small talk you do when you're nervous. Tom and I were doing it with each other, too. We were trying to make jokes about a silly thing Karl Stefanovic was trying to do to Lisa Wilkinson on the *Today* show. As the sun was coming up and peeking through the window, I was only thinking of Elsie. Was she up yet? Was she having brekky? Was she looking for her mumma?

Simon arrived and was excited, too. We talked about the day and what would likely happen. I had already had more of 'a showing' the week or so earlier and was starting to feel some cramping, like things were already in action and I was already starting to dilate. Even though I already said yes in the lead-up appointments, he again asked me if I wanted to have my waters broken to 'get the party started' (my words, not his). I now was so ready to have my baby. Yes, yes, yes.

We were given privacy to move through the early contractions. The midwife was just popping in and out as needed. Simon was watching the monitor from his office (I had one of those wide yellow elastic belts around my belly.) Slight contractions were coming and going but nothing too intense. After a few hours, we were again asked if we wanted to keep things moving to try to avoid maternal fatigue like last time.

Yep, we are ready. I gave the green light to the cannula and induction.

Just like we hoped and planned, this time was totally different. The nurses asked the anaesthetist to pop in for a chat. He was a confident man. When he offered to insert the cannula, I was also much braver this time. I asked him to put gloves on first. With the confidence he had in his abilities, he was able to explain why it was better he didn't. That meant I was totally okay with that now. We had autonomy in decisions – so far so good. In went the cannula, first go. No troubles. Here we go!

The contractions began very soon after and, at this stage, were still okay. I could breathe through them, knowing they would pass. Next, it was shower time and for a while the warm water was super helpful. The frown that grew on my face probably indicated to Tom when the shower was not so super helpful anymore. The midwife was in the room ready to help if we needed it. When I no longer felt like I could handle the pain, she reminded me of some options and I was able to decide.

At first I was standing, leaning on the back of a chair. Then I asked to get onto the bed sucking down that gas as each contraction became stronger. I said to the midwife I feel like I wanted to do a poo. Simon suddenly reappeared to see how things were going. He seemed happy to see that I was so far along. Our son was ready to meet us! Wow! 'He has a lot of hair,' said Simon. For the first time, I discovered what it felt like to have the urge to push. My body wanted to push. And I did. I was lying on my side to keep my bladder out of the way, with Tom at my head. With each push, I grabbed his tee-shirt, almost ripping it off. A few more big pushes and out he came.

And then our little Louis was on my chest with a blanket over the top of us.

My initial thoughts and words were, 'Is he okay? Is he alive?' As I'm writing this I realise this was my biggest fear, because I said it at Elsie's birth, too. Fear is a bitch. I was so scared that my babies would die in childbirth and yet I was never allowed to talk about it with the midwife. I was only ever worried about my babies, not me. Louis was fine. I was fine. Tom was fine. We all held each other and cried happy tears. This was the one and only time I saw my husband cry. 'We did it!' he said. Louis was so cute with a head full of dark fuzzy hair. He looked just like his mumma.

A happier little family

The next week staying at the private hospital, and the level of care and support we received, was amazing. We felt comforted and safe. It also helped that the food was very yummy and that Tom was able to stay with us. He stayed for the first night, but then I wanted him home for Elsie so at least she had one parent at home with her. And Louis and I were so fine on our own, in our own room, looking over an escarpment. What a great way to start out.

I was very specific about Elsie getting to meet Louis first, before any other family members. It was important to me that it was just the four of us, our happy little family. Tom bought Elsie in the very next night after the birth. She was in her PJs and dressing gown. I'd missed her so much in the previous 24 hours. I was already emotional but when I saw her walk through the door, my heart exploded with love.

We introduced Louis to his big sister. He slept through it. She smelt him and was inquisitive – until she went to kiss him. She licked him and said, 'Yuk!' We all laughed. Like most one-year-olds, she then wanted to play with all the controls and buttons she wasn't supposed to.

This time round, it was lovely having visitors. Sharing this wonderful moment was special. My family would bring Elsie in to see us, and she was starting to find it hard to leave at the end of the visit. It was time to go home – 'home time'. I was sad to leave this warm and safe space, and I would miss the daily visits from Simon. But at the same time, I was very excited to be going back home.

We were now a complete, happy little family.

By now you may have seen my social media profile pic of the four of us, taken while we were holidaying in Disneyland with Mickey Mouse. It's the happiest place on Earth, right? And the profile pic seems to back that up. The truth behind the smiling faces is actually a little different.

Things like this come at a cost – and it's not just financial.

Ask yourself ...

- If you have experienced birth trauma, how do you feel about your body now, and how does this affect your relationship with your partner? Do you compare your body now to how it used to be and mourn what you've lost? How can you take things minute by minute to cope?

- How do you feel about birth? How do you feel about sex? If you have experienced birth trauma, what experts could you approach to help if you do want to have a second child?

CHAPTER 7
THE COSTS

Don't get me wrong; the photo taken in Disneyland captures what was a very happy time. The smiles are real. The happiness is real at that very moment. But behind those grown-up smiles is the hard work and effort that goes into getting to that place (and I don't mean just the plane trip).

In this chapter, I'm going to try to provide some insight into what it costs to live every day with this type of birth trauma injury. Getting through each day the best we can involves a huge expense, including the emotional and physical costs. I'm also going to share the specific financial costs. Originally I wasn't planning to because I thought it would be a bit boring or not relevant. But after reading some comments on Facebook about a woman who successfully sued the very same hospital to cover costs from the damages caused by her traumatic birth, I realised that this is a hugely important topic to cover, too.

Why Disney?

As a young child I always dreamed of one day going to Disneyland. The decision for us to go with our little family was kind of made at the last minute. Not too long after the birth of our bubba boy, it was discovered that I had a non-cancerous desmoid tumour growing in my abdominal wall. Apparently, they can occur during pregnancy, though are very rare. Hearing this did make me feel like my body was never meant to carry and deliver babies, and like it had failed me, yet again. With another 'life's too short' reality check moment, we decided to spend money we really didn't have and take our happy little family to Hong Kong Disneyland before my surgery to remove the tumour.

Here is what it cost to get that Disneyland photo taken, with all of us in it. Tom and I had to plan the entire process out the night before (very unromantic). The queue to meet Mickey was always long. Tom would need to stand in line while I sat around the corner waiting for our turn. The photo needed to be taken first thing in the morning, when the prolapse isn't as bad. Mumma was the last to get out of bed and once dressed we all raced down to get it done.

I can't stand or walk (without pain) for longer than five to ten minutes at a time. If I'm standing or walking, I need to wear dresses only. Pants become too painful after a short while (even the loose, elastic-waisted ones). Gravity works against me. The more I stand or walk, the more both my bladder and uterus start to slide down and out of the vagina. Yep, the bladder pops out whenever it damn feels like it.

By the way, I was once given advice that I could just push the prolapsed bladder back up. *Gross*, I thought, *I'm not touching it*. Early on in the piece, I did give it a go in the shower one night. I was scared to do more damage so I was gentle. It didn't do a thing. So I tried pushing with more force next time and the time after that. I stopped once I realised that my bladder was never going back in with a simple push. My internal organs literally hang down and outside of my body.

As my bladder falls out of the opening of my vagina, I lose all core strength too, which leaves my tummy to 'flop' out. This is what makes wearing pants too painful. On a funny sidenote, I often get asked if I'm pregnant again, although only in the afternoons.

So that's what I was up against, and that's why some of the simple things such as getting a happy family photo taken come at a cost. It is also stressful not knowing when I'm going to be okay and when I'm not. It is unpredictable. Along the way we have learnt to implement what we refer to as 'workarounds' to make things like this photo possible, (I'll go into these workarounds and tips in chapter 9.)

On the daily, after Disney

For us, every day is planned in a similar way to the Disney photo. At the start of each day (actually more so the night before), I have to decide where I am going to 'spend my bisccis' (short for 'biscuits'). This is the phrase we use when thinking about where I am going to focus that small window of non-pain hours. Will it be watching my kids playing in the park or will it be trying to get dinner prep done? My days are broken up into sections of activity and rest, with lots of sitting and lying down. Any type of downwards pressure exacerbates the prolapse, with the simple things like vacuuming or simply bending down to pick up things from the floor making it painful.

And if the extensive planning goes belly up for some reason, I start to spiral into a flipping-flopping mess. I can't make decisions about what to do or how to prioritise. My head becomes a mess. The cost to my family is the flow-on effect on them. When it all gets too hard, I do nothing. Not plan A or plan B. I fall in a heap for a while, which means mumma is out of action. It is all left for Tom until I pull myself together.

Tom works full-time. He is also a full-time dad and husband. He has his own goals to pursue and is training to run his first marathon later this year. That's a busy day in anyone's eyes. On top of all of that, he also cares for me, and does all the 'heavy lifting'. He mostly attends to the waking babies at night, so I can get the maximum time being horizontal. The cost of that is he's always tired and, yet, he NEVER complains about anything. He gets up at 4 am to run, goes to work, and then comes home to help with the kids. He never complains that the house is a mess or we have the same meals on repeat, week in and week out. I know how lucky I am there.

The cost for me is the loss of autonomy and spontaneity. Anyone who has spent time with kids knows just how quickly they have a new idea and, all of a sudden, are running off to do it. This includes my two bubbas. They run around all day long, which is okay at home but, if we are out, Tom is the chaser. Even when we do stay home all day, there does come a point where I physically can't stand anymore. I push through most of the bulging feelings and think I have a high pain threshold for the physical stuff.

The biggest cost to me, Stephanie the person, is a bucket load of self-worth.

When it comes to the emotional stuff (and I'm having great difficulty even getting this out on paper right now), I try really hard at every moment to be the best mumma. I've already shared my vision of putting my baby in a carry pouch. I remember travelling all the way up to Sydney when I was 38 weeks pregnant to the Baby and Toddler Expo. I wasn't going to have a look around. I already knew exactly what I wanted: the Ergobaby carrier. They were selling them much cheaper there than in any of the baby shops. Baby was going to be close to my chest and I was going to wear her around all day long, patting her bottom and back. Just like in the hospital birthing class. That is what I was going to do.

Tom laughed at the dad on the box of the Ergobaby, saying he didn't look like he was loving it. Hubby was not so keen on wearing it and, yet, he was the only one who was able to wear it. I put it on once and put Elsie inside, just to get a photo of the happy little family. Then it went straight back to Tom. I was very envious of this.

I also imagined us going for walks along our beautiful local beach, chasing around in the park, exploring our amazing bushlands. None of that stuff happens the way I planned. I feel guilty for that. That is what hurts the most.

The headspace of longing for something you dreamed of but not getting it in reality, to remembering just how lucky we are to have bubbas in the first place, is exhausting. It means I discount or ignore my true feelings because I don't want to be ungrateful. At the same time, I really miss my mumma dream. I miss the really simple stuff: lifting my toddler into the cot at night, being able to lift them when they fall down, dancing with them, and lifting them in and out of the car. I miss the things that mummas do every day, as part of their normal day.

There have been lots of times when I've had no choice but to do these things. I just do it. And then the cost is to me. The prolapse continues to drop, feeling heavier each minute and then the pain travels to my perineum and eventually to my lower back. It's too late by this stage to do anything to feel better except go to bed – for the night. I also miss the really simple stuff for me: showering standing up at night, being fit, and being able to wear a tampon. I now have no choice other than pads. Yuck! It's like being a pubescent teenager again.

I no longer even have control over my bodily functions. Every cough or sneeze is a slight moment of panic. *Did I just wet myself?* I automatically cross my legs or sit if I feel the inkling of a sneeze coming. And winter sucks! Coughing hurts. The bladder yo-yos in and out with every cough. People think I don't want to be near them if they're sick because I'm a germaphobe. Nope, it's because of the cost I have to pay if I do get sick. Lots of pad wearing.

Oh, shit...

One of the more horrifying moments of my life more recently was when I was with my son at 5 am. (Yep, he's an early riser.) I was still half-asleep, kneeling on the lounge-room floor to change his night nappy, with only my nighty on. I get up to see a tiny poo on the floor behind where I was kneeling. *Strange*, I thought. I didn't think he'd done a poo. *Oh, shit, was that me? Did I just shit on the floor and not even feel it? Oh, shit, I just shit myself.* I had no idea. Scary shit, right?

I was frozen. I couldn't speak. I didn't tell anyone, not even Tom.

After Googling too much, I phoned Professor Dietz for HELP. He was sorry I was so stressed about it. Funnily enough, though, he did say it was 'common'. This could happen and does happen, and he said he probably should have told me it could happen. *Ahhh, yes, Prof, you should have.* I thought I'd made the prolapse worse because the day before I'd 'overdone it' that week – not by choice, Tom was away for work. I thought maybe this was the next phase of shit to deal with – literally. Good news (yes, there is some): it didn't mean the prolapse was getting worse. It can just happen as part of the prolapse.

After too many glasses of wine that weekend, I broke down and finally told Tom what happened. He embraced me so lovingly that he didn't need to say anything. He did eventually say, 'Well, thank goodness it was here at home and not at work.' Which gets me onto my next cost: the cost to my career.

Back to work?

By this stage I wasn't at 'paid work' anyway. I was at home on maternity leave as well as unpaid sick leave from the desmoid tumour. I loved my career. Over 15 years as a teacher, I had worked my way up and enjoyed the variety of the day. Going on maternity leave early while pregnant with Elsie was hard. I loved being busy and the spare time was hard to fill. Teaching was the thing I knew how to do with confidence. It was my life.

When Elsie was born, Tom was finishing his final year of uni. He'd studied computer science part-time while working at Qantas. He was entering his final exam period after six years of correspondence and on-campus study. The crescendo. It was all happening at once. With me not working, and Tom working on Thursday nights and weekends in a bike shop, money was tight. We had some savings stashed away from selling our Sydney house to move south. We lived off that somewhat during this time and were coping okay with the weekly bills.

Once Elsie was born, we used my maternity leave pay for the weeks it lasted. Tom finished uni and was now looking for work. It was the lead-up to Christmas and everyone was on the wind-down – certainly not looking for a fresh-out-of-uni developer. We went to his uni graduation and it was a great day. I felt proud as punch to be there celebrating this momentous occasion with the two loves of my life. Elsie slept through the whole thing (very unlike her). At the end of the (long but thankfully seated) ceremony, I saw I'd missed a call from a friend who was also a teacher at a local school.

After mingling outside with some friends, I phoned my friend back and she told me she had an offer for me to work part-time the following year – sharing a class with her. Fun! I wasn't ready to go back to work, though. I was a new mumma with an eight-week-old baby. Then I did the maths, and worked out Elsie would be a bit older by the time school went back the next year. And then I added in the fact that neither of us had a job or money coming in. Final answer? I had to say yes.

It was now time to work out with Tom how this could actually work for me, and for our family. Oh, that's right, how am I going to stand and walk to teach? I didn't really know at that stage but knew I literally could not afford to say no. We visited the school that afternoon and met the staff having their Christmas luncheon. Everyone seemed very nice. It only took one comment about me coming back to work so soon for me to freak out (in my head). Was this going to be too soon for Elsie? Was I being a bad mumma?

I had lots of long conversations with Tom about this over the next few weeks. I felt so much guilt, and worried I was leaving my girl too soon. I thought I could always just try it and back out if it was too hard for me physically or emotionally. Then there was a huge shift.

When Tom said he wanted to be at home with his baby girl, too. That made everything easier. It now sounded all that much better in my mind. I counted the days I would be at work and took out all of the holidays. It added up to not too many days apart, and it was school hours with minimal travel. Elsie has two parents who love her. We could both care for her. Tom and I could both work a couple of days a week and both care for our baby. This was great team work. And it worked – somewhat.

Working it out at work

Tom did all of the heavy lifting to make sure I could physically do my job on those two days. This meant lots of prep leading up to those days, and mumma resting a lot. The cost to me being at school all day was that, when I got home, I had to be horizontal (most of the night). Tom would bring Elsie to me. I could still play and feed and all of the mumma things, I just had to do it lying down. I managed to hide my pain at work. Because I was still breastfeeding, I had to pump at lunchtime, which was good for me – I was able to sit and reset too. Teaching older students that year made it all the more doable. Still, lots of workarounds were needed.

I also became close friends with a very special teacher. One day she saw I was in pain and I decided to share a tiny bit with her. She totally understood what this meant for me, having had firsthand experience with prolapse in her family. Her support made the world of difference, even if it was in a world of our 'secret women's business'.

The following year looked a little different. I was no longer team-teaching with my buddy, and my new job share had some medical issues of her own. Unfortunately, the comments and ridicule she received from other mummas cemented my feeling that I could never let on about what was happening to me. Some of those mummas were super judgmental and cruel. That year I was also newly pregnant with my second baby, and so I was already the worst person for planning to leave to have my baby halfway through the year. I made it to the end of those six months – just.

Financial costs ... and then some

Tom and I were okay with the fact that financially we would be at a 'stand-still' while I was on maternity leave. In our pregnancy planning phase, we knew we wanted to maximise the time we could have our children at home with us. We also knew that it would be temporary, and then we could be back earning two full-time salaries. To prepare for this, we had saved over $20,000.

The prolapse changed this plan, though. The medical bills were piling up. They were not in the budget. The $250-plus for each specialist visit or 'chat' to get referred to another specialist to pay another $300 was all adding up. Also not in the budget were costs like a lighter pram (purchased because I was not able to lift the one we had into the car), the pessaries, shower chair, the nanny for support, counselling or the three-weekly physio appointments. This is not an extensive list of things, but I think you get the idea.

During that second year of me being back teaching, Tom also found a programming job close to home. It was part-time too. We both worked the opposite days, playing tag team. The new job meant more money, which sounded great in theory. But then things became hard. Tom was no longer at home to do all of the heavy lifting. We had a little extra money coming in, but now less time for help and less time to do the things we needed to keep the house ticking over. We chose to hire a nanny to help. She helped care for Elsie when we were at work, and she also helped me to attend appointments and with the day-to-day stuff. It wasn't really financially affordable, but we couldn't afford not to.

Tom's work was becoming busier so he started working full-time. I was struggling. Now pregnant with Louis, I needed Tom more and more. This cost him at work. He was trying hard to be everything to everyone and finding it hard to concentrate with being so tired from everything. Just before Louis was born in July, our nanny went to India. While Louis's birth was amazing, the issues in the early weeks with him feeding and sleeping were not. I finally understood how to breastfeed, and felt I could do it this time. But he would feed, cry, vomit, do explosive poos and cry some more. This happening compounded all the other stuff. We were trying our best, but we were drowning.

We got some help and support from a paediatric/neonatal nurse (which my mum and sister paid for). Her name was Marnie and she runs a service called Whispers Cottage that helps families within their own homes. Very quickly she became like our guardian angel, helping to trouble-shoot everything. Was it reflux? Feeding too much, not enough? Colic? Tongue tie? Tummy issues? Wind? Just the newborn baby thing? Louis didn't sleep and cried non-stop for the first few weeks at home. I wasn't getting any sleep and didn't feel like I was bonding with my son. The tongue tie was confirmed, which was affecting his feeding, and one of our friends rescued us by lending one of those side-swinging baby cradles, which worked for a little while. But we needed more help with the daily living. I was sure our nanny was due back by now. Turns out she was, but her short reply to me after sending her a pic of the kids and asking when she was back in town was something like, 'Hi, I'm back. Had a great time. Sorry. I can't help out anymore. I need to focus on study now'. While I was lucky to have secured a day for Elsie at a local family day care while our nanny travelled, we still needed daily help in the house.

Oh. Right. Shit. What do we do now? We looked into a few different options, but nothing suited. Nothing was okay. I wanted someone I could be comfortable with. I was in a very bad way and didn't want to feel like I had to put on a brave face for a stranger – or, worse, for someone we sort-of knew. I felt like a complete and utter failure. I could not fix Louis. I could not physically care for my kids. The pain was hanging around and not giving me any reprieve. Tom stayed home a lot with us during this time. The ultimate cost of this was his job.

The cost to me was my mental health. Looking back now, the pressure I put on myself was immense. I was trying to be normal and do normal things. It just wasn't working. I was calling Marnie every day, and sometimes three or four times a day. I started looking for more help in the usual new parent 'go-to' places, such as the Karitane parenting centres and Tresillian family care centres. No places were available in these services for months (and months). Eventually, Marnie suggested a place in Sydney that had a mum and bubs unit. It made reference to God in the name, so I initially thought this was not really what we needed. Then I looked them up and gave them a call – I was desperate by this stage. Both my parents had exhausted their leave from work to live with us.

Once I was on the phone with the manager at the mums and bubs unit, and as I started describing what it was like at home, I ended up in tears within the first few minutes. I talked about my physical pain, my guilt and the feeding and sleeping issues I was having with Louis and how I hadn't been able to get to know him yet because of all the constant crying. There was certainly no woowoo in this house.

The manager told me that had a vacancy within the next few days. She said they were a little different in that they allow mums to stay up to three weeks. *Good*, I thought. *I can stay a few nights, get on track with Louis's needs and head back home.* Then she told me part of the program included a check-up with a paediatrician. *Awesome*, I thought. *Fix him up and I'll be better.* It all sounded super easy. All I had to do was get there – until, that is, they told me that Elsie was not able to stay with us. It was just for Louis and me. I had no real choice here. I had to deal with leaving her at home for a few days, and it was so hard. It was a very emotional time, but it had to be done. Tom drove us up while Elsie was at family day care. The love from our amazing carer there did help. I knew Elsie was very happy at family day care and would be fine with her daddy, too.

Getting more help

Arriving at the mums and bubs unit, which was attached to a hospital, was daunting. The foyer was nicely presented with images of families with new babies. I didn't really pay too much attention to anything else. I was scared of Tom leaving us. We were so far away from home.

The first interaction with the nurses was nice and terrifying at the same time. They introduced themselves then whacked on some rubber gloves to search my bags. What for? I wasn't going through customs. I was so confused. Tom and I sat there with Louis in the pram and watched as all of my things were searched. The nurses didn't really explain why they were doing it, telling me it was just part of the admissions process. After that, a long afternoon of initial appointments followed, and lots of questions to answer about mental health. Then it was time for Tom to head back to pick up Elsie from care, but I wasn't ready. Here I was, in this strange place with mums and bubs I didn't know, and I was shit-scared.

Luckily, I met a nurse that afternoon who I connected with straightaway. She was so loving and very chatty. She talked me through how the program worked, telling me that, for the first week, Louis was going to sleep in the nursery at night, the second week it would be one night on (sleeping in the room with me) and one night off, and by the third week he would be back in the room with me. Oh, and I was required to attend counselling sessions each day. *Umm ... thanks, but no thanks.* I only wanted to be there for a few days until Louis could see the paediatrician so he could be fixed and we could go home. My baby only slept with me. I was breastfeeding and I trusted no-one other than Tom to care for him. And I didn't need counselling. I was just tired and in pain.

'I think I'm in the wrong place,' I told her. 'I don't belong here.' The penny had finally dropped that this was not the usual mum and bubs unit.

'Well,' she said, 'you're here now so how about you stay the night, keep Louis in with you and ask for help if you need it.' Okay. There really was no choice. I certainly wasn't going to get Tom driving another four-hour round trip with Elsie in the car at 7 pm.

So I was shown to a room, which was nice, clean and comfy. Louis and I had our own quiet space to hang out in. All my food was prepared and I had nothing too much to do or worry about (other than the overload of being a new mum again). I said a quick hi to the other mums in the lounge area, and saw some dads were staying, too. They all seemed nice enough, but I chose to stay in our room that night because I didn't feel at all social. I missed my husband and I missed Elsie. I felt super guilty for not being there to tuck her in and kiss her good night.

Throughout the night, the nurses helped me. Louis had recently had his tongue tie snipped so I expressed and fed him with a bottle. (I was expressing at every opportunity I could.) The nurses were going to help me get Louis to reattach to the breast the next morning, but I was still worried that it was something in my milk that was making him sick. His poo was always explosive and mucus-like. Add in his non-stop crying and I felt that it must be because of how I fed him or something in my breastmilk.

The next morning, I was feeling anxious about not knowing if I could feed him 'right'. Was he getting too much air in? Was this what was causing the wind and crying? Was the flow too fast or slow? I was so confused and could not make any decisions. About anything. At the time, it felt safer to keep expressing and giving him a bottle because then I could know for sure whether he'd had enough or not.

During the day, all the mums disappeared on and off into different parts of the unit. Some were talking with doctors and others went to counselling. They all spoke very openly about their own struggles in the lounge room. Some mums did not feel love towards their babies, and I didn't feel like I could relate. I loved my kids so much. This was clearly not the place for me. I didn't go to any of the sessions they suggested. After Louis's paediatrician appointment, we were going home. The paediatrician only visited once per week, on a Wednesday. It was only Tuesday, which meant if I wanted to see him, we had to stay another night. Not loving it, I did it. I did it for Louis.

Over the day and night I got chatting to the nurses while feeding Louis or eating dinner. They offered a great ear to share things with. No judgments. The nurse who I'd clicked with the first afternoon was working that night and asked if Louis could hang with her while I caught up on sleep before going home. She promised to bring him to me at any time of the night if he was upset.

Initially, I could not settle. I was worrying so much. All the what ifs? and how abouts? were going through my head. What about poor bubba? Was I a bad mumma? What was I doing? After a shower and expressing as much as I could, I watched some TV. I then must have fallen asleep quickly because the next thing I knew, Louis was back in my room starting to wake up. It was 6 am already ... the difference I felt for having slept was amazing. The nurses came in to help with latching and, just like that, he was back breastfeeding. Yay! I felt somewhat more normal that morning, like a real mumma again.

Louis's appointment with the paediatrician was also that day, meaning we would get clear direction and then it would be home time. I phoned Tom to tell him about the good news with feeding. He was happy for me. He was managing at home fine (and probably better with just the two of them to worry about). Elsie was happy hanging with her dad. Tom asked me if we could leave the pick-up until the weekend because things were really stressful at work and he could not take any more days off. I was really sad but put on my strong brave mumma voice and said yes.

Later that day I told a nurse about the conversation with Tom. I started to cry. I cried and cried, and cried some more. I thought I was crying because I felt sad that he didn't want us home, and that I felt rejected by my husband. It was super sad. Hours of talking (and crying) with her, however, helped me understand that the tears were not about the phone call with Tom. They were from two years of sadness from the birth trauma. I finally lifted the lid on my 'bad-arse mumma', 'I can handle anything' attitude and was able to let myself feel the pain.

The costs

The pain of feeling like a failure. The pain of not thinking I was good enough. The pain of loss. I felt a huge loss about not having what I'd always dreamed of – the plan, the woowoo. It was gone. I had no control. I had no control over anything. I had no control over my experience, my body, my physical feelings, and my sadness. This was why I was working ridiculously hard to control and fix every other aspect of my life. I had to fix my son. I had to fix our family.

Something shifted after that afternoon, and I realised the first week in the unit was just the very start. Tom came up that weekend – not to pick us up, but to stay the night. I now knew I needed to stay and do some hard work, and that this was the place to do it. I didn't love it. But I was starting to see how the trauma had affected me and therefore the people I love most. I was doing this for them – and, as I would learn in the following weeks, it was for me, too.

During the three and a bit week stay, I learned more about myself than in the first 37 years of my life. I attended all the sessions and wanted to do more. Learning how our thoughts and values can dictate our lives and, ultimately, our happiness (or even ability to function) was fascinating. Sharing things openly in a safe environment was a good thing. It really helped.

Not being at home with Elsie for three weeks came at a huge cost to me. At the time, the guilt and fear that she would remember me not being there for her was so hard. I worked through it with a lot of help and guidance from the professionals. I would be teary every time I said her name. It certainly helped that Louis was doing much better, too. The specialists I talked to thought he had an allergy to something in my breastmilk, possibly the lactose, which I learnt is naturally produced in the breast – meaning I couldn't do anything to stop it.

So Louis was now off the breastmilk and on a special allergy formula, which reduced his vomiting and crying. He smiled for the first time during that stay, something he had never done at home. My maternal exhaustion was also much better and I was able to make simple decisions again, like what to eat for breakfast. This stay didn't 'fix' us 100 per cent, and it wasn't meant to. It did teach me that it was okay not to be fixed or the fixer, and that recovery was a process. And that process could be long or short. I just had to trust the process and try to be more fluid in my thinking about certain things. This was a good way to cope.

Back to the happy little family

Things shifted back at home for us. Tom and I were talking a little more openly. This was not easy and we needed to work hard at it, but it meant we were in a much better place than before I left. We were starting to find more and more 'workarounds' to help manage each day – or each moment when shit hit the fan. Remember the 'hour by hour' thing I mentioned in the previous chapter? It worked for us.

By now, we were heading into the end of the year. Things at work for Tom were intense. He still needed to be around to help us a lot at home because we still didn't want to share our load outside our four walls. We weren't ready to ask for the help we needed. We didn't really know what to ask for. Tom and I are proud and private people. He never was able to open up to his boss about why I needed so much help. He wanted to protect me, and we thought it would be easier to just knuckle down and work harder. Clearly that didn't work. And things didn't work out with Tom's job. It was too hard and too late to try to explain. We were back at square one.

Opening daddy day care (even though we hate that term)

So Tom was out of a job and I certainly wasn't coping at home with both kids all day. So we swapped roles again, with the idea that it would be much easier for me to return to work full-time than stay at home. No lifting babies all day, along with all the other heavy lifting jobs required while Tom was at work from 8 am till 5 pm. Tom knew how to raise his own children. He was open to the idea of being a full-time daddy. Work would be easier for me. The school hours were shorter than his office hours, I was still close to home, and school holidays would be paid. I knew how to do my job – well – and it would be good for my mental health to feel like I was achieving at something. It felt like a no-brainer. (Well, that's what I told myself at the time, like I had a choice.)

Returning to work was very different this time, however. I had a class of much younger students, and this just naturally asked for a lot more moving around from me. After only about three or four weeks in, I realised that this was not going to work. I couldn't talk to my boss, because she was new and we were unknown to each other. How the hell do I tell my boss what help I need without telling her my vagina was so broken? We didn't have the kind of relationship to be able to do this. The kids in my class always came first – at the expense of myself, my physical needs, my pain. This cost was also carried by my own kids at home. While I was working full-time, my two babies only ever saw their mumma lying on the couch when I got home. I barely moved – only to eat and go back to bed and then back to work. The weekends were just to simply recover physically from the week at work. Tom was doing everything. No-one loved anything. The job was costing me my family.

Eventually, I had the courage to speak with my direct supervisor. I told her very little, but she was really lovely and didn't ask me to explain. Her support was amazing. We talked a lot about the different workarounds, and I tried them all. I made sure that I took on extra admin roles to overcompensate for doing less physical roles. Under no circumstances did I want to be seen as getting special treatment.

The cracks started to appear anyway. I tried hard to ignore the comments and rumours from parents and staff when they saw me sitting down to 'teach' sport. I took my profession seriously and knew I could not continue on the level and standard I set for myself. I'm pretty sure that leaving the classroom to run to the bathroom six times a day would not be regarded as okay. But neither was wearing wet pads until lunchtime either.

Towards the end of the term, Tom was offered a job – one he could not refuse, and one our family could not refuse. He was being paid substantially more than before and we could now afford to have someone help me at home during the day.

School's out, for good

My trauma and damage has cost me professionally and financially. Not working as a teacher now means that I'm not able to continue on my chosen career path. Not working in any paid profession means I no longer have the ability to save for retirement. No superannuation, no long-service leave.

So what were we meant to do now? While Tom was earning enough to be okay right now, we would never be able to pay off our mortgage. We were only making the minimum interest repayments. Everything that came in, went out. We were stuck ... or were we?

Ask yourself ...

- If you have experienced birth trauma, what are the costs of this trauma and damage to you, and to your partner and family? How has your life changed? And how does acknowledging these costs and changes help you with dealing with your trauma?

- How much do you like to stay in control? Do you focus too much on presenting the perfect family/couple/person to the outside world? How is that working for you?

- Regardless of your situation (whether you have experienced birth trauma or are not yet pregnant) are you holding on to grief from your past? Is pushing it down working, or can you start to acknowledge it and work through it? Who could help you with this?

CHAPTER 8

NEVER TRUST A LAWYER, THEY SAY ... LEGALS AND INSURANCE

After Elsie's birth, we were told by our midwife that everything was 'normal' over and over. It was said so many times, we believed it. Even if it didn't feel right, we didn't question her authority on this at the time.

My mum was not buying it from the start. This caused us unnecessary conflict and overall was a hard time for my relationship with Mum. Mum was trying to tell me – no, she actually told me outright – that what happened to us was anything but normal. Mum worked with nurses and ex-midwives who agreed with her. I certainly never felt normal again. Even so, we were working super hard to try to get to that normal, or what normal to us looked like now. We were struggling with everything. How could that be normal?

At the end of one of my regular exercise sessions at the physiotherapy centre I was attending three times a week, I walked out the rear door to head back to the car. Elsie threw something out of the pram and I stopped to pick it up. As I stood up, I saw a sign for a law firm. It was right next door to my physio. Funnily enough, I'd never noticed it before. From very soon after the birth, my mum and a few other close women had been telling me that we would have a legal case against the hospital for what had happened to us. I would shut them down every time they brought it up. Legal action seemed a bit ridiculous for something that was 'normal'.

Well, I'm here now, I thought and before I knew it I was pushing the pram through the front door of this small law office. Maybe they could put this to bed once and for all. I spoke with a young guy for about half an hour. He said they would make contact with me if they thought I did have a case. I left that day thinking I would never hear from them again. But I did. The very next morning Lady Lawyer, a nice sounding lawyer, phoned me to make a time to meet. We met at the same office the following week. We spoke for over an hour. She took copious notes about what we talked about. I thought she was a great listener, and I felt like she cared about what happened to me.

Mum just might have been right. Tom and I then met with Lady Lawyer, and she took us to a barrister's office across the road from her office. He was a stern older man – not too old, though – and he seemed to know a bit about this medical injury stuff. He asked some hard questions and it made me cry, even though I didn't want to cry. For some reason I wanted to be tough for him, and show him that I could be strong to 'fight' if it was to be the case. He thought we had a clear case against the hospital.

Speaking with Tom about this was stressful. He wasn't so sure. When it came down to it, neither was I. We had never heard of anyone liking the legal process. We've only ever heard of the heartache and that saying 'never trust a lawyer; they are all the same'. Not Lady Lawyer, though. She seemed different. She was all for helping us, she said. I was very clear from our first meeting that I wanted to get

Never trust a lawyer, they say ... legals and insurance

this resolved so I could move on, but without it costing me my marriage or family life. It was already hard enough. She reassured me that they would only make contact with me when needed. Her firm were also 'no win, no fee'. This was the only way we could even consider this.

I understood that, and left it alone until they did contact me. I was asked to obtain all my medical records from the hospital and get a report from my treating doctor, detailing the injury and details. So I gave Lady Lawyer the contact details for Professor Dietz. I then received an email from the firm saying that the report from Professor Dietz was ready but it was very expensive. She was trying to 'work something out' at her end, knowing we had no spare money left.

That was the last time I heard from Lady Lawyer. On the last line of her email, she'd written, 'Wish you all the best, Steph. Today is my last day working here'. I phoned Lady Lawyer the minute I read that last line. But what about our case? What happens now? Is it finished now? Lady Lawyer reassured me that the case would continue with another highly skilled lawyer who worked on medical cases. The second lawyer was on leave but we would meet her in a week or so. Lady Lawyer was true to her word and the report came through. It was emailed to me from her assistant.

Reading that report from Professor Dietz, I was in shock. I had no idea it was that bad. Although I didn't understand all the jargon and numbers, it was clear that Elsie's birth was very risky. I presented to the hospital that night with so many risk factors that there was already an over 80 per cent chance the birth would involve complications to me and/or her. You don't need to be a statistician to work out that those odds are not great. No amount of smelly candles and calm breathing were going to make that percentage okay.

I was furious that such a high risk of complications both for me and my baby had been allowed. There was every chance we were not going to leave that hospital without suffering some of those complications. This was like waving a red flag to a bull. Sorry, that's NOT normal.

Time for action

Stick it to 'em, I thought. It was time to tell the hospital my birth and situation was not normal. In my mind, we were all going to sit down and finally hear the truth about my birth, find out from the hospital why it went the way it did. This was not going to happen to one more woman. Instead, I had another big learning curve ahead of me. The law does not work that way. I don't know why, it just doesn't. There was no meeting, no debrief, no truth.

I met the replacement lawyer for the first time in a meeting back at the barrister's office. Some time had passed since we saw him last. He was still certain the case was strong with a positive outcome. That was also the last time I saw him, however. He retired not long after that meeting, meaning we had a new lawyer and a new barrister.

I met the new barrister on my own. Tom couldn't keep taking time off. I liked this new barrister. She was from Sydney. It was sold to me by the firm that she was THE go-to person for medical negligence cases. She seemed to really know her stuff, even down to the brand of dress I was wearing (they help with relieving any pressure on the tummy). She talked fast, but I could keep up with her. I was brought to this meeting in the pretence that I would share my story with her. So she could understand the matter.

On the oversized boardroom desk were five or six massive files, and not all of them belonged to me. They were for the other mummas the firm was working with that day – all from the same hospital. She told me that they couldn't bring a class action against the hospital due to the varying birth trauma causes and damages, but the hospital was the common factor. She was going to review my matter and contact me when it was time.

We didn't hear from the firm or the barrister for a long time. The only contact we had was via the law firm's legal assistants. Looking back, the assistant wrongly answered questions and set too many incorrect expectations – which led us to what would be our final meeting with law firm number one. This was a meeting between Tom, the lawyer and barrister, and myself. The assistant told me it was so the barrister could meet Tom and take his version of events ready to file the matter with the courts.

That meeting went nothing like what we had been led to believe. Tom did not get a chance to give his version of events. The barrister wanted to know what we thought was going to happen once we filed. The main outcomes we wanted were to be able to replenish the copious amounts of money we had spent on therapy, have enough money to continue therapy and be able to pay our mortgage (because by this point I had attempted both part-time and full-time work and now knew I wasn't able to go back to teaching).

Most importantly, however, we wanted to make way for change. I wanted the hospital to recognise that our experience was not 'normal'. I wanted an apology. I wanted to be assured this was not going to happen to anyone else. Very bluntly, the barrister told me my last two requests were never going to happen. The only outcome from this I could hope for was a small sum of money to 'go away'. We would be lucky to pay off some of the mortgage after all the costs were taken out.

I liked her honesty, but didn't like what she was saying. I was also baffled as to why this was the first time I was hearing anything like this. What would be the point in speaking out if nothing was going to change for anyone else? I sure as hell won't be allowing my daughter to think that having a baby means you break – and that's normal.

One fatal word

When we thought it could not be worse, the barrister then asked me if I would have elected for a caesarean birth. I said yes, had I'd known all of my risk factors. 'No,' she said. 'Would you have chosen a C-section as your first choice?' I said no. Before I could even continue, she interrupted and said, 'There it is. We are going to have a very hard time with this case because you are against caesarean births.' Not only was my case going to be hard to prove, she then started telling us about all the risks we would now have to take on.

She told me the law firm representing the hospital and their insurance company would 'tear my integrity to pieces' because I went on to have another baby. She then asked if we owned our home, and I told her we did (along with the bank). 'Okay,' she said. 'If you lose this matter, they can take your home.' *No way!* No-one would allow their kids to be homeless – right? We had just moved from a villa into our first home, next to a playground, with no steep driveway. I was no longer a prisoner trapped inside all day. We could now have the option to walk a few metres to let the kids play in the park. We could not allow this to happen. This is not what we signed up for.

This apparent major shift in our case had both Tom and I in shock. We didn't really know what to say now. Was that it? Done? The lawyer from the firm told us what our bill was to date and we only had a few days to decide what we wanted to do because the time frame for statute of limitation was fast approaching. A bill, for what? I thought this was 'no win, no fee'.

Wrong. So wrong. You do have to pay for disbursements. Apparently, details on this were in the contract I signed at the start. I didn't remember seeing or signing any contract that talked about paying for disbursements. It certainly was never discussed or explained to me. The bill was ours no matter what. We now owed close to $10,000 to a law firm who only had led us to believe that we had a very strong case for over two years. And that case was now falling apart all because of one simple answer: no to a caesarean.

How the fuck did we end up here – $10,000 worse off than we were before we started? What had I done? I started this, even when Tom was hesitant. And now I'd made it worse. I'd said the word 'no', so now we owed all this money we didn't have. We couldn't even borrow that amount from a bank. How the fuck could I fix this now?

Tom and I left that appointment both very quiet. We didn't have a chance to speak. He was due back at work. I had to go to the hospital for an appointment, because the tumour I'd had removed previously required me to have genetic counselling. I went into the appointment feeling like shit. I wanted to crawl into a hole and die.

The intensity of the genetic counselling was unexpected. Counselling sounds lovely, like it would be helpful, right? In this case, very wrong. The lady told me shit no-one wants to hear – that I could have passed this genetic mutation on to my children, that I had a very high chance of getting bowel cancer, that it all depended on the result of a blood test. In the meantime, she wanted to book me in for a colonoscopy. *Take it easy, love.* I thought. *Let's just wait until the bloods come back.* I was very dismissive of the seriousness of this. The only thing playing on my mind was how I was going to pay $10,000.

The conversation with the barrister kept playing around in my mind. It was a real head fuck. How can it all be over just because I would not have opted for a caesarean first? She had totally missed the fucking point. It was never really my choice to begin with. Natural childbirth was the only thing I knew. I didn't decide. It was told and sold to me. We were never allowed to talk about C-sections, because you only have them when things go wrong. When you fail 'natural' birth and have no other option but medical intervention. That was never going to happen to us, that's what we were told. 'You will be fine', 'just breathe the baby down', 'create a relaxing environment', 'trust your body' and 'your birthing partner will know what to do'. It's all natural.

When the trust is gone

Who in their right mind would choose to go against the people they trusted with (more than) their own life? They hold the most privileged position. I trusted our midwife with everything, my living and breathing heart and soul. It makes no sense that I would invest so much only to 'choose' to go against everything she had told us about birth. What bullshit.

I needed to talk with the barrister some more. I needed to share with her my real thoughts about this and how I thought she had missed the mark. I wanted to make real change, not just cash. I phoned her office and had someone return an email saying she was not allowed to talk with me without my lawyer present. What? I was done with the lawyer. She hardly spoke to me for two years and it certainly felt like I'd been lied to or somehow fooled. The barrister seemed to be the only one speaking any truth. I had no faith in my lawyer anymore. Not being able to speak with the barrister, however, I did try contacting the lawyer so she could give me some sort of permission to speak with the barrister.

They lawyer's auto email reply said she was going on holidays for two weeks and to contact blah, blah. Yep, it was confirmed. I was so done with her. On one hand, she was pushing for me to make a decision to file the matter with court or not and yet, on the other, was not there to help me. After an email to her boss, my phone rang later in the evening. It was the lawyer, just about to leave for holidays. Left with no choice, I told her what I wanted to tell the barrister – that I thought they had it all wrong, and that they were missing the much bigger picture. All of a sudden, the lawyer came up with an idea to help the case. She suggested we obtain an independent obstetrician's report. If that was in our favour, we could proceed. I just needed to hurry up and make the decision.

I thought we already had such a report from Professor Dietz. He had written reports and answered questions as requested. The lawyer explained that because he was my treating doctor, these reports were not enough. The report needed to come from someone I'd never met. Oh yeah, and she told me that I would have to pay approximately $4000 upfront to get it. She was only telling me this now?! After all this time? We didn't have that amount of money. My gut was telling me this was not the way to go. Any thread of a relationship or trust with this lawyer was gone. We were done.

Of course, this didn't change the fact that we still owed them a pile of money. I could not make any clear decisions about this before speaking with more people. More professionals. I had so many questions left unanswered, and I searched high and low for answers. I was so stuck. I was then kindly pointed in the direction of a law firm in Newcastle that specialised in birth trauma. I spoke at length to someone about what mess I was in. She was going to send me a follow-up email about what we could do next – which would, of course, involve spending more money.

Number one takeaway from this? A promise of 'no win, no fee' will never mean you don't pay for something.

Next please ...

While waiting for the email from the Newcastle lawyer to arrive that week, I was on Facebook. I'd been off all social media, as directed by law firm number one, but was now just scrolling through other people's posts. I discovered that a relative (by marriage) was also in the law game and had, in fact, worked at the same Newcastle firm I'd contacted. Was this a sign or merely a coincidence? I didn't really care at this point. I had to speak with him. I wanted some real, honest answers and opinions. He, too, didn't have a good feeling about the way things had been managed thus far, telling me that independent reports should always be sought first, to even decide if there was a case or not. We spoke at length over the next week, and he also spoke with Tom. We decided to get him to take over. If anything, it was going to help us clear the debt with law firm number one – or so we thought.

An independent report was sought. It, too, strongly reported that my pregnancy and actual birth were very much mismanaged. I had way too many risk factors to have been allowed to birth the way I did. Finding this out in hindsight made me feel terribly sad. All this damage, pain, hurt and suffering could have been totally different had I been seen (and heard) by someone else. The preliminary conversation already costs $2000+. To get the actual report was going to be a further $4000 or $5000. Oh my god! Who has this type of money just lying around to pay for medical reports?

It was now decision day. Do we keep digging this hole deeper into debt, in the hope we would be able to recoup some in a settlement? Or do we jump ship now and try to find a way to pay back all this money? Far out, it was so stressful. It was taking its toll on me, Tom and our babies. This was not cool. This was not how we wanted to be. Shit was already hard enough. We just wanted to get on with living – the best way we could.

It took hard conversations with family and friends, and multiple counselling sessions for me to be able to make a decision to proceed or not. I then had this great idea to take the story to the media and request payment for it. That way it was like two birds with one stone. We could clear our debt and also help other mummas. Win–win. And a major TV network showed great interest in the story (more on this later in this chapter).

So I made that hard phone call to law firm number two to tell them we were not going to move forward with the case. I was very honest and upfront about the fear of digging more into a debt hole that could never pay back. As supportive of our decision as he was, I could tell he was also disappointed – for us. He had a great belief we would be successful in a large win. 'Great beliefs', however, don't pay large debts.

Number two takeaway from this? A lawyer will NEVER give you a guarantee of a win. Not even a percentage of likelihood. They just can't.

One door shuts, another one opens

So with no way forward on the legal side, I had to keep searching for a way to get my story out and help other mummas. My 'never die trying' attitude does help sometimes.

To help explain this part of my story, let's go back about 20 years to when I was buying my first property. My mortgage broker, Paul Wright, told me that it was a must to have the right level of insurances, including income protection insurance. At the time, I was young, fit and healthy. I decided I didn't need to pay for something only older people needed. This became a big lesson learnt a few years later when I had cancer – and had no insurance and almost no income. Silly me. I do let my broker tell that story to his new clients. I hope they listen to him, unlike me.

I got older and a little wiser, and was buying a different property. My mortgage broker said it to me again. This time I listened. He put me in touch with Julie Van Meegen, a great financial advisor who did all the hard work for me. I had no real clue what I was doing. Again, I never thought I would need income protection. My options for cover listed so many exclusions for anything relating to cancer, because it was now a pre-existing condition. What I later learned is that is also excluded me from claiming due to any stress, anxiety or depression. They were all now considered 'pre-existing' from the cancer days. Who wouldn't be bloody stressed during chemo? Anyway, I never thought I would use it, but decided to follow the advice of the experts and sign up for cover anyway.

It was only during a review meeting with my financial planner, Julie, that I remembered the first lawyer's assistant telling me to apply for any insurance policies I had, now that I was no longer able to work. I asked if this birth injury would be considered, because it wasn't cancer or anything like that. Julie was amazing and helped me start the process. It took a little while to gather all the required paperwork and reports and, once I submitted it all, I forgot about it. I'd never done anything like this before. I'd always remained working in some capacity, including through cancer treatment.

A few weeks later, I received a call from my insurer. They had more questions and required further documentation. Once that was submitted, my claim was approved and the waiting period began from the last day I was able to work. I had to wait three months before the first payment but, by this stage, it didn't matter. We were just so grateful to Paul for suggesting it and Julie for making sure I was covered for this type of thing. This payment is how we now survive today. It is nowhere near my earning potential if I was still teaching, but it is so much better than the alternative – nothing.

Are you covered?

As I've mentioned, another lesson we learnt following Elsie's birth was to make sure our private health insurance was up to date and covered us for everything including childbirth. This time I ticked the right box, just in case, and this level of cover made the world of difference during the second time around for the birth and beyond. We could never have afforded that stay in the mums and bubs unit. (I think the total for the three weeks was around $15,000.) And not having to worry about the money aspect while recovery was the focus was fantastic. So our insurance policies and claims were taken care of, but we still had the major issue of lawyers wanting to be paid. Insurance money didn't cover that amount.

Spread the word?

With recouping costs via the legal route now off the table, the only thing left was the potential TV deal. I'd been in touch with a producer a number of times, who wanted more info, photos and contacts – ASAP. I provided everything requested. (They always like to work quickly, like there is some urgency.) I spoke with Professor Dietz and few other key players, and they were all keen to help get the message out there. During one of our last conversations the producer did say that her executive producer didn't love the use of the word 'vagina'. It didn't sit comfortably with him, and thought it would be too much. *Good*, I thought, because if he didn't like it, then nor would a lot of other people. Good or bad, it would get the conversation going at least.

It was in that same week that I watched an episode of the show I was in discussions with. The piece was about some football fan and sex. I didn't really watch from start to finish but got the gist. Football and sex gets ratings, I guess. It was very tacky. The reporter was tacky. *No thanks*, I thought. This is not what this story needed. Our broken mummas don't need this shit.

So where to now?

So now I was left with no story, no legal case, and no money to pay this huge debt. I felt so lost. I felt so responsible for what was happening. I was sliding down the sadness slippery slope with no way to stop myself. I had hit rock bottom – again. Each night after just making it through the day and dinner, I would sit on my phone and play Tetris. I hate that game. But it was the only thing keeping me distracted enough from my own thoughts.

It was very unlike me. I loved playing with my babies on the floor. Now I was happy letting them watch *Bluey* on ABC Kids as long as they liked. Tom had to keep telling me to put the phone away and help put the kids to bed. Some nights I could and others I couldn't. I don't think he really knew what to do. So he let me be. He let me keep playing. I was lost in my head and thoughts. What was I going to do?

The counselling sessions were great while I was there, but by that 7 pm time, I was only okay if I was playing Tetris. It worked so I kept doing it. I was on my phone a lot. This then became the morning routine, too. I was using it to cope with the physical pain as well as the pain in my heart. The whole situation wasn't right. I kept asking myself, how could we be worse off for trying to get help and help others?

When reality hits you like a box of Cornflakes

One morning my two beautiful children decided to make a lovely art work for me – out of a whole box of rice bubbles, a whole box of corn flakes, a new jar of honey and a roll of baking paper, all over the kitchen floor. I came out from the toilet (where I had been hiding and playing Tetris) and saw what was in front of me. 'Look at what has happened,' I said to them. Really, I was saying it to myself. The realisation hit me like a tonne of bricks. What the fuck was I doing with this life? I was losing it. I cried with them and then we all laughed. Something had to give.

It was time to find a 'workaround' to this problem, just like all of the other hurdles we had found workarounds for along the way. This was no different, just a mega $10,000 hurdle. And a bigger hurdle required some bigger thinking.

Ask yourself ...

- How much experience have you had with the legal system and with 'no win, no fee' cases? Would you read all the fine print and question every piece of advice you were given? Or would you trust these experts were here to help you?

- Are your insurance policies (such as income protection and health insurance) up to date? Do you know what you are actually covered for and whether it will be enough for what you might need? Who could you ask for help with this?

CHAPTER 9
MY WORKAROUNDS

One good thing came out of playing Tetris all the time. I was on my phone a lot so I was seeing and reading more too. Since being banned from socials by law firm number one, I had only been using LinkedIn, reading articles about education and tea (my two previous careers). I scrolled over an amazing picture of a serene beach. And then it kept popping up in my LinkedIn feed. It was from Andrew Griffiths, someone who I had admired for some years now, since my small business days of having a tea retail and supply start-up with Sharn, my bestie. I had followed him on podcasts and watched the talks he gave, and saw he was running an author's academy in Bali for people wanting to become authors. None of these two things applied to me. I wasn't thinking of becoming an author and I didn't love my first visit to Bali decades ago. It just looked like a really nice place to escape, not an answer to the big workaround I needed ...

But before I get into that in more detail, let's look at some of the hurdles and workarounds I already had in place.

Living with a prolapse

First I want to run through the actual physical damage from this traumatic birth, what this means now and why we even need to work around these hurdles. I think being able to communicate this, and so encourage other women to speak out, is important. I would also like to add these hurdles and workarounds are on top of what is already a bullshit-hard job. Being a first-time (and second-time) parent is exhausting – lovingly exhausting, but exhausting.

Here is my official medical diagnosis from Professor Dietz:

> *Stephanie is presenting with a markedly symptomatic three compartment prolapse, the bladder leading against the background of severe ballooning and a complete right-sided avulsion ... this means the right-hand side was disconnected or torn off the bone ... the 4D pelvic floor imaging confirmed the clinical examination findings ... bladder prolapse, minor descent of the uterus and a complete right-sided pelvic floor muscle tear.*

To put this in terms I understand, my pelvic floor is only half there. The right side is simply 'flapping around in the breeze'. The left side is carrying the load, doing all the work. No wonder it gets tired trying to hold up all those organs.

From that very first appointment with Professor Dietz, there was always talk and an expectation about this end goal of having some kind of repair surgery, reattaching the right-side muscle back to the bone. That sounded pretty simple, and then I'd be fixed. Yay! As I've mentioned before, having the surgery just meant we had to be sure we were finished having babies, because having surgery was pointless if then taking the risk of it relapsing. After Louis was born our happy little family was complete. So very complete. It was time to get that repair work done and get back to being the old me, the mumma I wanted to be.

It was early January and some preliminary testing required prior to surgery – called urodynamics testing – had to be completed first. By the end of an appointment of being catheterised, poked and prodded in the vagina and anus, I received one of my biggest blows of all time: 'Stephanie, I'm very sorry to have to tell you this, but the damage is too extensive. The conventional surgery option would likely have a 90 per cent failure rate.' I was very much advised against surgery and told that 'no current surgical method is available that can effectively reconstruct a pelvic floor muscle that has been damaged to such a degree'.

So this was the biggest hurdle – bigger by far than our legal bill. How do we get around this one? I've always been both a practical and creative thinker. If something doesn't work, just try something else. And if that does not work, keep trying until you find that thing that works.

This time, however, we had reached the end of the road. We had nowhere else to go, nothing else to try to be fixed. It's funny (but not haha funny) how we adjust to things better as time goes on. It was so hard to hear that news, but we had to move forward. And so we started getting even more creative.

Physical workarounds

The following provides a list of hurdles we have discovered along the way. More importantly, it also outlines how we have got around these hurdles. The workarounds are not recommendations coming from someone with a medical or professional background in pelvic floor function. They are just what have worked for us as a way of moving towards being as normal as we were before the birth.

During the process of final edits for this book, I thought I'd start sharing a few of these workarounds on a private Facebook group I created called Tips & Tricks for living with POP (pelvic organ prolapse). I didn't want other women to wait months before this book was released to get some additional support. And what started as a few friends has grown exponentially with each week. A minimum of ten women have been requesting to join per day, from all around the world. This tells me this is much bigger than me, and much bigger than I could have ever imagined. And to know it is so big and yet still so taboo feels overwhelming. I move through this by focusing on the small wins: helping at least one more woman who may be living in silence.

Pain when walking or standing

Choose where you need to use your non-pain period each day. Mornings are best for me and pain increases with the hours in the day. I try to have planned breaks of sitting or, better yet, lying down during the day (although this is not always achievable). Meal prep, for example, is done in the morning or even on the weekend when I have more help at home.

Showering

We bought a plastic chair for the shower. This helps me at night to wash my hair or shave my legs. Trying to lift one leg up makes the prolapse so much worse.

Baby tools

Our first pram was too heavy for me to lift so we saved up and purchased a much lighter one that has two separate parts to make it easy to lift. And forget the nappy change table. We had a foam mat on the floor to reduce the lifting up and down. It is easier to sit down than try to lift all day.

Food

I try to eat foods high in fibre to keep stools soft. And I take dietary fibre and a probiotic to avoid any straining when I eat junk food. Pushing and pressure are no good. Water is good. Finding that sweet spot of not too much or too little can be a bit tricky. We have tried a range of the meal prep kits such as Hello Fresh. They made things easier in the sense we didn't have to think (and they are very yummy), but a bit more prep was required compared to what we normally did. The best thing that works for us now is a two-week meal plan. Each fortnight, I sit down and decide what to have, only buy ingredients for those meals and prep for those meals. This takes away the element of having to think about what to have each day.

Toilet

I recently watched a YouTube clip on how to 'use' the toilet with a prolapse to avoid pushing down. (The process is hard to explain so check out the clip by going to YouTube and searching 'how to empty your bowels without straining'. You'll see you have to make some weird sounds, but it works.) I only do it at home. I use this technique in conjunction with a step stool to raise the knees. I also try to know where the next bathroom will be, and Apps are available that can tell you this. Just like the kids, I go before we leave the house and when we arrive at our destination. It might be a bit over the top, but I go often to avoid wetting myself. I also always take a spare change of clothes for me too, in case I don't make it – or the public toilet is not okay.

Exercise

Exercise is my way to feel better both physically and mentally. As someone who once loved triathlons, I miss running a lot! Finding exercise that works for me has taken a lot of trial and error. I now know sitting is better than standing, and lying down is better than sitting. And finally finding the right exercise physiologist has made all the difference. My program is tailored and adjusted each week. My exercises are done lying down on a 'reformer' bed. Knowing how to actually do a pelvic floor 'lift' was imperative, and this was done with specialist 3D scanners and medical instruments so I could physically see on the screen what a good lift looked like and felt like. (Turns out it was very different from the ones I thought I was doing right.)

Getting out of bed or off the floor

Instead of sitting up like when doing an ab crunch, to get up I roll to the side and flip onto all fours, and then use my legs to push my body up so no pressure is placed on the tummy. And I always think about engaging the pelvic floor before getting up.

Lifting little people

This is a hard one. We worked around the nappy change thing, but lifting in and out of the cot or pram is unavoidable. It was easier when they were super little, and Elsie ended up in a 'big girl' bed before she was two, which meant no more lifting. Now they are a little older, Elsie does not need any help and I get Louis to climb up as much as he can, and just support him. When they cry I sit on the ground to hug them. I do lift when I can, but try to get them to climb up on a chair so I'm only lifting halfway, and then we sit on that chair to cuddle. And I always brace or engage my pelvic floor first.

Washing

For a little while I would manage each load of washing by walking a few things at a time to the clothes line. Then I got smart and purchased a portable line with wheels. Then I got even smarter (with the help of my amazing exercise physiologist, Karlie) and purchased a washing trolley just like the one Nanny used for her Hills Hoist.

Making the bed

This is a job I leave for hubby. Or I ask my family to help when they visit. (We have found that family and friends like to feel helpful. When they are asked to help with something specific, they are more than happy to do so.)

Period

That time of the month is horrible. No more tampons, because they simply can't stay in. Pads are the only option. I didn't swim for a week out of every month, until I was put onto the new swimmers and undies that are designed for this very thing. I only use the swimmers right towards the end, for the last day or so of my period. A few different brands sell these specialised undergarments now, and I personally use Modibodi.

Cleaning

When we can afford it, we use Airtasker to get someone in to help me vacuum, mop and scrub the bathroom. The best lifesaver for me was the robot vacuum. Two small children sure do make a big mess when eating three times a day (or more). Our poor robot vacuum sure does get a workout. Along the way I also discovered that a steam mop is much easier to use than a conventional one, with less friction and so less effort required.

Strange but super helpful

I was struggling at night-time bathing and the clean-up afterwards. Trying to carry the dirty pile of clothes around to the laundry was not helping my symptoms. I asked Tom a random question: to save me walking all the way around to the laundry, could he just cut the door in half so I could throw the clothes into the basket from the hallway. He looked at me strangely, and then did just that. He created an internal barn-style door so no-one else has to know but us (until now, anyway). The point here is to try to think outside the box (pardon the pun).

Pain management

I have avoided the big gun pain meds from the GP because I didn't want to add another layer of complexity to this already hard situation. I have wrongly used self-medicated legal pain meds in the past (by this I mean wine). That only works for a very short period of time. I'm not drinking like that anymore after I had one glass too many one day and the pressure on the prolapse from vomiting far outweighed any benefit of numbing the pain. Again, sitting is better than standing and lying is better than sitting. Being horizontal is the best thing for the prolapse, and the longer the better. This may not be practical but it works for me. We have discovered along the way that saying I'm in pain doesn't really help – anyone. So we've come up with a scale: 1 to 4 means I'm okay but should start thinking about our next rest, 4 to 7 means I need to take a break for a bit, and

8 to 10 means I'm done, and you need to take over until I'm okay again. I have recently also asked the GP about different pain meds. I'm thinking about trying a pain patch, but am still unsure. I have used massage and acupuncture in the past but suspect it was the laying down that helped more so than the therapy.

Now the real heavy stuff: the mental and emotional workarounds

Dealing with the physical stuff is one thing. The hangover effects of the emotions, however, are huge. And a lot of this is also because it is kept silent. Until now, this was a secret only Sharn, Tom and I really understood. These physical workarounds have been very helpful to me, and to us. It is much easier for me to focus on the 'fix' (aka the workaround) than it is to actually deal with what this has done to me as a person.

The one thing I will say about dealing with the mental and emotional pain is that finding a good counsellor is so important. No – make that finding an *amazing* counsellor. It has taken me a while and a few different attempts to finally find a woman who has been truly amazing. I try to see her regularly – well, as much as the funds can stretch and when there is a spare appointment. She is so wonderful, which means wonderfully busy, too. She also put me on to the Headspace app. I would like to say I use it as much as possible because I know it would help, but I often fall asleep too easily at night. I'm still working on giving myself the permission to use the app at different times of the day.

Back to thinking big: Bali and being brave...

I didn't find that author academy in Bali. It found me. It wasn't what I was looking for at the time. Then, I was always looking for answers, for money, for ways to fix the problems. This shift from trying to fix everything to simply finding some emotional and mental resolve was life-changing. I didn't need to fix the $10,000 lawyer bill, because I couldn't. I didn't need to fix the prolapse, because I couldn't. But I could certainly change how I thought about all of this. It was my resolve I was looking for the entire time, not the fix. How do I stop this hurt and sorrow I'm feeling over this traumatic birth? So I did a very brave thing. I asked Tom if I could go to the authors' retreat in Bali – and said, 'by the way it's, like, next week'. He laughed and thought I was joking at first. He then quickly worked out that even though it sounded like one of my craziest ideas, I wasn't joking. Not one bit.

This was not an easy time for us as a couple. He said no. For the first time in our relationship, we disagreed on something so strongly that we couldn't even find a middle ground. At every chance, I would bring it up and try to convince him it was the best thing for me … only I did a crap job at it. I couldn't find the right words to say how important it was going to be for me. I'm sure I made out like I just wanted to escape my life.

I kind of did in a way – not escape the love of my kids or family but escape my own thoughts. The thoughts of doom and gloom. That my life had only become wiping up poo, being in pain and playing Tetris.

I touched base with Andrew Griffiths a few times via LinkedIn to chat about Bali. I knew I could not afford it. We didn't have the cash just sitting around. And then all of a sudden everything started to fall into place. I started getting the right words out to Tom. I started telling him how much this would change me, how much I needed to get this stuff about this trauma out my head and heart. I love that he found a way to say yes – even more so because he probably didn't really want to, but did anyway. That is true love right there. We managed to work out a few deals with the money side of things and I was off.

Okay, I've just made that all sound so much easier than it really was. The guilt about leaving my kids, the money, Tom – it was all playing on my mind. Bali was just calling me louder. I had to follow this.

Bali has now come and gone.

The pivotal shift in me has been truly life-changing. I still can't believe what it has done for me. This was the best workaround I have ever done. This was echoed just three days after coming home. We were all in the kitchen, just doing our daily thing, when Tom came up to me and said, 'You took that Tetris lady to Bali ... and brought my wife back.'

It says it all, right?!

Ask yourself ...

- How used are you to finding workarounds rather than fixes in your life? What workarounds do you think you could benefit from adopting right now?

- How can you change your thinking, rather than change your situation?

- What big move could you make in your life, to perhaps change it completely? Who do you know who could help you be brave enough to do so?

CHAPTER 10
MUMMA'S BACK – TO BREAK THE CYCLE OF JUDGEMENT AND SILENCE

I was back from Bali and I was also truly back – me, Stephanie. I was seeing things very differently, and with clarity and purpose. I was able to know that feeling of success again. I could do something and be good at it again. The prolapse played no part in my goal for this book being written. I didn't have to consider any physical workarounds. I could sit and write a book.

Writing this book has lifted the lid on the silence I'd placed myself in for almost four years. For the first time, I have opened up and talked to people honestly about what happened to us and how it affects all of us on a daily basis. This has helped me feel more genuine, more like me. I think I've said the word 'vagina' more times in the past few months than I have in my lifetime. No pretending anymore – that was exhausting.

So now, have I 'bitten off more than I can chew'? I made an (unspoken) pledge to my daughter that I would write this book and be the change maker she needs. But how do I, this one woman band make real change? Writing a book is one thing, one very small part. This is much bigger than just me and this book.

We need to try to better understand the reason behind the silence of many mummas first of all. It is always helpful to find the cause before trying to find the right action needed to make positive change. I can only think back to my own reasons for keeping silent. The two most impactful ones are in Fleetwood Mac's 'Everywhere' song from 1987. This, a favourite song of mine, talks about falling and not knowing what to say, and being too proud to get the words out. These two reasons ring true to me, and both help explain why I never spoke.

My silence around my trauma has been just that. I had no words to say. So many times, I have opened my heart and mouth and nothing came out. Or if I did try, it came out all wrong. And so I just went straight back to pretend mode. It was easier that way.

Being told it was all normal by my midwife, someone of such authority, made me believe it for a long time. I believed that what I was experiencing was just part of being a first-time mum. Having this belief meant I didn't know how to admit that I was broken. My birth wasn't normal like I'd been telling people, even my mum, all along, and I was too proud to admit that I was wrong. I thought it would mean that I would also have to admit fault in some way – that it was my fault that my 'smart-self' let this happen, that I somehow should have known better.

And therein lies the problem: just because we are women, we are expected to know how to do the big stuff, like birth a baby. I've read and heard so many people say just trust in your body, because it knows what to do. And if we don't know, we are expected to find out on our own. While researching for this book, I have seen this type of messaging aimed at women more than ever before, mainly in social media posts. A very strong push and message to women is out there that it is their own responsibility to be armed and knowledgeable about childbirth. I have even seen an analogy that went something like, 'You wouldn't go and fly a plane without studying first, so educate yourself and have a great birth plan'.

Sure, the idea of being informed and educated makes sense to me. But this push to make it solely mums' responsibility does not sit right. It makes me feel very stupid. I thought I did educate myself by reading books, listening to podcasts, going to those 'natural' birthing classes and asking lots of questions along the way. Is this message saying that I didn't do it right or enough? When I really think about it, these analogies are so unrealistic. Being a pilot takes years of both study and real practice. You don't have the option of 'practising' your birth before you give it a real go. When I read posts like this, they again make me want to be silent.

Like I've said, it's much easier to say nothing, to not go 'against the grain' and speak out. A few times I have responded to posts like these. I have tried to say that I did educate myself and still experienced birth trauma – so a 'foolproof' birth plan is impossible. I was trying to allow for mums to have a balanced view on all birthing methods and ideologies. But oh the judgment! I received so many responses from what I can only describe as activists for 'normal/natural' birth, and they didn't want to hear anything other than natural childbirth ideology.

The judgement files

We all judge. Judgement is a tool we use in life to make decisions. In that way it can be helpful. Judgement is no longer helpful, however, when we pass it on to others in a negative way. I think nine times out of ten when people feel judged, it's in a negative way. I certainly felt the judgement from those comments – like I was trying to do a bad thing, and sway mums away from the ideology they were strongly advocating for. This is anything but the truth.

I want first-time mums to be able to feel comfortable with asking questions and being inquisitive about this birthing space. I have discovered that it is, in fact, very complex. There is just so much to know. Our medical professionals study and practise this for years, and the most we get is a few hours in a class (if we are lucky). If mums are afraid of being judged in a negative way, they are likely to stay silent.

Finding out more is also the responsibility of everyone, not just the pregnant mumma. We need to be working together to give unbiased information about childbirth that is true and factual, still with all the love and 'woowoo'. I trust this will take some time and a lot of work. It's a big job, but if we don't start somewhere, nothing will ever change.

The time for change is now. This brave mumma is the advocate for change, to help break the judgement and silence cycle.

This needs to happen for all the mummas out there – the ones who are nodding as they read this, the ones yet to become mummas. Then for my family. My husband and my children. They deserve their wife and mumma, and for their wife and mumma to be okay with not always being okay, to be honest and truthful in life, to speak up and not to be afraid of the judgment.

Most importantly, I'm starting to break this silence cycle for my Elsie. She will never have to go through this. I will not allow for my baby to have this happen to her as a mumma. (I write this with tears streaming down my face.)

Mumma's back – to break the cycle of judgement and silence

Ask yourself ...

- How often do you judge other women and their parenting choices? Have you caught yourself thinking bad thoughts about a woman feeding her baby with a bottle rather than breastfeeding? Or for going back to work too early? Or for not going back to work? Have you stopped and asked yourself where these judgements are coming from and who they are helping?

- What have you stayed silent on but could speak up more about? What thoughts and fears have been stopping you?

CHAPTER 11
ADVOCACY

Advocacy is in my DNA. I've always gone 'in-to-bat' for the underdog. I'd always managed to find that 'special something' in the kids I taught who had the most challenging behaviours. They were the ones I loved working with most. I was their advocate and their voice, for them and to them.

Even when we were first told that we did not make it onto the midwife-led program, my questions were around why? If everyone was so in favour of this program and my mumma neighbour we spoke to said you basically had to book in when you first pee on the stick, why was it only available for a select few?

At the time, I was told it was because of funding and resources. Simply not enough midwives trained to this level were available to expand the program.

This didn't make sense to me at all. Why should some mummas have access to this special group over others? Why are we creating this divide in a public hospital? I remember asking the first midwife what I could do to advocate for more funding, to have more midwives available, to stop this being for an elite group only. Even if this meant we were not able to be part of it this time, but maybe for our next baby.

Little did we know at the time, but being part of this group involved meeting certain criteria. Certain risk factors are considered less favourable, and mummas with those risks factors were supposed to be rejected or transferred off the program to obstetric care. Guess what? I had a number of those risk factors and was still allowed to stay on the program. Where was my advocate? Who was looking out for me? (I honestly don't know the answers to these questions.)

Sticky social media...

As I started writing this last chapter, I got into a sticky situation – one I placed myself in without really thinking too much about. I made a comment on social media about what was meant to be a positive birth story. The problem was it wasn't the mum herself posting. It was posted from the company selling the birthing ideology and methodology she used. I commented that mumma was very brave for sharing, go her! I also added that because of the way it was shared from the company's page, that it sounded 'salesy'.

Clearly the company didn't agree with this 'salesy' comment, and responded to tell me so. But they didn't stop there. We both replied a couple more times. I tried explaining that I didn't mean 'salesy' in the money sense. I was commenting more on them selling an ideal birth, and the idea that their one method was going to give women the 'best birthing experience' (their actual words). After that, they commented on me not being respectful. I was at a loss. The interaction was going against everything I'm trying to achieve here. I'm trying to allow for the bigger conversations to be had about childbirth in a respectful and supportive way.

It helped me realise that I'd missed a step. I'd created the Bravemumma social media platform and I knew this book was on its way, but my messaging and use of words was not clear. Looking back, I realised using 'salesy' and commenting on that story wasn't ideal. So to avoid that mumma thinking or feeling my comment was anything to do with her personally, I decided to privately message the company. I knew I wanted to respect that mumma, and also knew I needed to respect *this* mumma. I had to advocate for me and mummas like me.

I explained that I, too, am a mumma and I had been through a traumatic birth. I was not talking out of school, only from my experience. My birth didn't work out the way I'd hoped. In the end, they said my comment would just be deleted. I agreed for them to delete if they thought it would be upsetting to that mumma. My gut feeling is my comment was going to be upsetting to their bottom line or their beliefs about their method.

That was the big question I now had. Why are we so hung up on holding our beliefs about childbirth so closely and so strongly? And when do we realise holding them so closely means we feel we have to protect them at any cost – through actions such as deleting people who don't agree. Acting in this way means the much-needed conversations stop right there.

My sister was trying to help me navigate through this sticky social media situation I was in. I needed a sounding board to make sure that I, too, wasn't holding on to what I thought to be the only truth, and that I was in fact able to hear what others had to say. She reminded me of a conversation we'd had before Elsie was born. She said when Tom and I returned from the birthing classes retreat, she'd asked me what we did because these types of private classes just weren't around when she gave birth. (She has two kids who are much older.)

When we were talking about how we were going to just 'breathe the baby down', and I was explaining our calm birthing plan and not using pain medications and so on, she remembers telling me I was kidding myself if I thought birth wasn't going to be painful. She even remembers the hurt on my face when she laughed out loud when I said they were not called 'contractions' but 'surges'. I don't even remember the conversation at all.

From my uni days, I understand that we are part of certain discourses throughout our life – meaning we align ourselves with a particular practice and way of thinking we believe in. And to be able to believe in something, we need to learn about it and feel a certain way about it; we need to 'buy' into it. And to be able to first buy into something, generally someone needs to 'sell' it to you. In the example of our birthing classes, we were 'told and sold' the ideal that our birth was going to be very special, calm, magical, beautiful and, most importantly, natural. Who wouldn't buy into that? This ideology was only reinforced by the messaging in the books we read and the conversations we had with our midwife. It all sounded like it was only ever going to be like this.

Here's the tricky part. For some women, this natural ideal is very possible. I saw the families who appeared to have an amazingly beautiful birth with little or no medical intervention, pain medications or complications. I'm sure the companies who still sell this 'natural' ideology would say they only have success stories. Maybe that is all they really know. Come to think of it, we have never spoken to anyone from the company we did our classes through, so they would be none the wiser about how our birth turned out. And this is probably part of why they can say theirs is the 'best' birthing method. They only know what they know, too.

All this is why, in the end, I decided not to post anything more on that social media page or send any more messages. I had to spend my energy getting the wording right for this book first, for the mummas who would be interested in knowing more about what happens when the natural childbirth ideology does not turn out as expected and hoped. I was totally respectful of this woman and her business and certainly wasn't about to say the method doesn't work for some – well, let's be honest, a lot of – mummas.

Part of why I haven't said anything untoward about our first birthing classes until now is because at first I thought we just failed this whole natural childbirth ideology way of birthing. I thought perhaps we didn't do what they said enough, didn't listen to the meditations enough, didn't 'breathe the baby down' enough, didn't have enough buy-in. I thought maybe we *wanted* the 'woowoo' calm birthing experience so bad, but were too uptight or worried too much to achieve it.

This is why it's so important to try to break this secret women's code about not saying anything untoward about natural childbirth. Within the close circle of women I know, they have not shared their traumatic stories because of the types of things they were also told during this style of calm birthing classes. 'Don't listen to any "horror" stories. Don't let the lady down the road tell you about her friend's daughter who had a terrible experience.' And why?

Because of fear. We don't want to be scaring women about what *can* – no wait, *does* – happen. Every time I hear the words 'horror story' I cringe. I want to scream at the top of my lungs, 'They are not fucking horror stories! This is my story. They are our stories. They are real. Horrible, yes, but not made up or glorified.' Until now, I have told my story to no-one in any great detail, let alone anyone thinking of having a baby. I don't want to be seen as trying to scare them either.

I'm now working hard to help break this silence, my own silence. I have had two very different birthing experiences and I would never put one against another. I can now only wish that I'd had someone to help guide me through what happens when your plan does not go to plan. Or someone to say, 'It is okay to be scared, let's talk about that some more.' I only wish more unbiased information was made available to women about this very thing.

My gut feeling is that part of the issue underlining this pitting of vaginal versus caesarean birth is the push in society for everything to be perfect. We all want the best. Not what is simply the best *for us*, but THE very best. We feel the pressure to have that picture-perfect moment, captured for all to see. This once very private life-experience, which traditionally was women's only business, has become big business. Dads have only been permitted into the delivery room since the 1970s (with this being a more widely accepted practice from the 1980s). In those days, people didn't really talk publicly about their birth experience and now it feels as if every second mum on Instagram is sharing their professionally made birth 'movies' or professional birthing photoshoots – from the actual delivery room.

Not everyone will agree with what I'm about to say here. And, in fact, they might say the exact opposite as to what they have seen on TV. But I really only see one image of childbirth represented. And I'm not talking about the acting on telly childbirth; I'm talking about the 'real-life' photos and images we see. We only seem to see the picture-perfect births, the ones that went to plan. We see the amazing photo capturing that moment the head crowns the opened vagina (I remember the presenter in my birthing class calling it a 'blossoming flower', explaining that our vaginas would naturally unfurl like a flower opening).

We have no perfect photos of my birth, no perfect pictures of me losing so much blood or being put back together with three layers of so many stitches. The midwife took a few photos of Elsie wrapped in a blanket on my chest. They show me in shock, and part of Elsie's scalp removed. The blood on my cheeks was not from me during her birth, but from her bleeding head. The suction from the failed vacuum tore the skin off her scalp. The bones have been permanently damaged too. A 'kiwi-cup' sized ring can be felt under her hair. It was traumatic. Seeing your newborn baby like this was traumatic. All the while, remember, I was being told it was all normal. We were simply lucky to have her here. Well, this is not true. Yes, it's true that we're lucky Elsie is here with us. But when did birth trauma become normal? Since when was it okay for our advocates to simply dismiss any trauma as 'normal'?

It simply is not okay. This is obviously not an issue that only happened to me. I'm not alone. However, in the weeks and months after the birth, I never felt so alone. That was until I discovered the Australasian Birth Trauma Association (ABTA) through Professor Dietz.

I am so grateful for Prof Deitz, Elizabeth Skinner and Amy Dawes for creating this organisation for mummas, just like me.

ABTA provided me with a place to find a lot of information and support services after the fact, and I am now part of a private support group, one that is built on safety and trust within ABTA. Simply talking with other mummas and knowing I'm truly not alone here was both reassuring and devastating – devastating because the member base is only growing, and fast, which seems to me like the wrong direction. Surely we should be looking at prevention rather than picking up the pieces when it's already too late? How do we do that? What will it take for this to happen? Where to from here?

> **Ask yourself ...**
>
> - Have you ever found yourself in a sticky situation on social media? If so, how did you resolve it? Why do you think people are so quick to defend their particular corners?
>
> - What images of 'normal' birth do you see? Do you see any variation from the 'picture-perfect' ideal?

WHERE TO FROM HERE?

*I*t was only halfway through writing the previous chapter that it hit me. *Oh my gosh, what had I done?* It was only through thinking and re-thinking and then writing about the social media incident that I realised. It wasn't the 'salesy' part of my comment that was the issue. It was those few little words I wrote before the word 'salesy': 'it's a shame it sounds salesy'. What was I thinking? I just did the very thing I'm trying to stop. I passed the judgement of 'shame' on something a company was doing. Of course they were 'selling' an ideal birth; that's their job, right? Who was I to say that was a shame? Why? For who?

The real truth of it is I was sad. I felt it was a shame – a shame for me, that it didn't work for me. I didn't get that ideal birth. I bought what was sold, and I still didn't get to have it.

Now I was left wondering ... how was I going to succeed in starting healthy, honest and unbiased conversations about childbirth, when I did this without really knowing at the time? How are we ever meant to be able to make change when we are not truly conscious of what we say and how it can affect others? When we think we are entitled to comment on how *we* feel, without any consideration.

Today I'm showing up and telling my truth. I got it wrong. I probably shouldn't have said that it was a shame. I am sorry for any offence. I can't take it back, any more than I have already tried, but I certainly learnt the lesson it has given me (even if it was the hard way). Throughout this book, I've only really talked about all the problems with birth trauma.

Here is the start of the solution. Think before you speak. Sounds simple, but it's not that easy, clearly! I didn't even realise what my words were doing until days later and after a lot of reflection. Know what you are saying to others and how your position sways the conversation. Soon-to-be-mummas – read, read and read some more. Not just the 'woowoo' books but also the medical journals and papers. Ask questions, and then more questions to more people, not just those within your own circle – who often will only confirm what we think we want to hear.

Be curious about all aspects of childbirth. Don't put your head in the sand and only believe one way (because you are only told and sold one way). Still have all the love and wonder of meeting your baby, AND also know there are two ways you'll get to meet your baby. It will be either through a caesarean section birth or a vaginal birth. Both do have medical related risks, so know what they are, and understand what they are – for both methods. Seek the answers to uncertainty. Find someone who can answer your questions honestly and give you the chance to move through any fears around those risks for either method.

Be aware of whatever 'camp' the expert you are talking with might belong to, and how this might mean they can only give you one perspective – and are likely to be quick to defend that position. Be sceptical about facts and statistics that seem to support the outcomes of one method over another, aware that the shroud of 'secret women's business' can keep some women – those who had negative outcomes – silent and absent from the statistics. Also be aware that hospital records don't always reflect what actually happened (as was the case with mine), and so these absences and silences also skew official statistics.

Tom and I didn't know what we didn't know. We asked questions and didn't get answers. We left it at that. We didn't feel we had the power to challenge the answers given (even when they didn't feel right at the time). We believed everything told to us. We were smart, educated people but, as first-time parents, we were also blindsided by what we didn't know. We put all our trust into one person and, therefore, her beliefs and biases too. We put all our trust into one 'natural' childbirth ideology, at the expense of finding out anything about anything else. We can now only wish we had access to a book like this book beforehand, so we could find out more and make informed decisions prior to the actual labour.

My one big wish for this book is that it opens up conversations. When a woman first becomes pregnant, I hope she can start an open conversation with her GP about how she thinks she'd like to birth her baby, and then be given unbiased information about both vaginal births and caesarean births, and information that takes into account that individual woman's circumstances and risk factors, and looks at why one method might be considered more suitable than the other, with the choice ultimately being hers – without judgement. Importantly, the open conversation would include the known medical risks for both methods, to close the current gap between some who argue 'I don't think women need to be given all the risks and complications' and those how argue 'We might need to scare women'. (These quotes are taken from opposing sides in a 2018 article from SBS's *The Feed* titled 'Birth Wars' – see www.sbs.com.au/news/the-feed/when-experts-disagree-the-best-approach-to-giving-birth for more information.) A comfortable middle ground needs to be found, rather than women feeling like they're stuck in a battleground.

Throughout a woman's pregnancy, I hope changes helped along by this book mean she's given ample opportunities to talk through any uncertainty about information and any of her fears about the unknown. And that these conversations remain unbiased and non-judgmental, with her needs and her baby's needs the only focus. I know this perhaps sounds like a long shot and a bit 'pie in the sky', but I also know it is achievable, because I was able to experience this with my obstetrician at our second birth. And I am truly grateful for that.

Finding my voice and advocating in this area is the happy ending of this book – not winning a huge case against the hospital or successful surgery to get back to what used to be normal. I've found a way to change my thinking, find our new normal and break the silence around birth and birth trauma.

That is only step one. This book is planting the seed for change. It alone cannot be *the* change. It now starts with me and what I think and say to others. It starts with the Bravemumma-hood. It starts with the professionals in this space. It starts with society. It starts with you. Brave YOU!

FAQs

Q. **What does a broken vagina actually mean?**

A. Medical terms and jargon can explain what a broken vagina means. In everyday words, it means that my bladder and uterus are no longer supported by the pelvic floor muscles to stay up in place (where they are meant to sit). They push or fall down the vaginal canal and out of the vaginal opening.

Q. **How does a vagina 'break'?**

A. The injuries to my pelvic floor muscles were a result of the use of forceps during my labour. It has been documented that the forceps would have disconnected or torn the muscle off the bone.

Q. **Why not just have surgery to get it fixed?**

A. No current surgical options are suitable for this extensive injury. The only current options have a 90 per cent failure rate within two years post-surgery, and this would also mean a hysterectomy.

Q. **Can you still have sex?**

A. All I can say is that our intimate life has never been the same since.

Q. How did you go on to have another baby then?

A. This was one of the hardest decisions. We consulted with multiple specialists to see if was even possible to carry a baby full-term again. And then had many, many consultations about how I was ever going to feel like I could go through childbirth again. It took a lot of deliberating, fact-finding and self-healing to be able to consider another baby. The logistics and more details are in chapter 6.

Q. Why haven't I heard of this before?

A. One thing I have learnt is that it's very common to have injuries resulting from childbirth – both from vaginal births and caesarean births. I have also learnt that birth trauma comes in many forms. Not all women suffer birth trauma and yet so many do, only they are not able to speak about it.

We have this 'secret women's business' code, which means we don't talk about taboo topics like this. There are so many complex reasons why; however, I do feel we are starting to shift away from allowing this taboo to stop us from speaking up. That is what this book is aiming to do – start conversations. It doesn't always have to be picket lines and protests. I mean the simple 'tea and chat' types of conversations within your own circle of trust.

A NOTE ON MEDICAL TERMS

I hadn't even heard of so many medical terms before giving birth – and important terms, relevant to my experience. Some of these weren't even in the books I read or spoken of in the birthing classes we attended.

Even some of the resources and glossaries I look at today exclude some important ones, such as episiotomy – described as a 'slight cut' during my birth. For the record, an episiotomy is a surgical cut to the perineum and posterior vaginal wall to make more space for the baby to pass through the vagina. Episiotomies require suturing after the baby is born.

Even Wikipedia has three definitions within vaginal childbirth – a spontaneous vaginal delivery (SVD), an assisted vaginal delivery (AVD) and an induced vaginal delivery. And within the reading I've done, natural childbirth means no medical intervention at all: no drugs, and no anaesthetics. Instead, the woman relies on techniques such as relaxation and controlled breathing for pain.

So many terms aren't even discussed, and so many have varied definitions, so I'd recommend looking at multiple sources. But you don't know what you don't know, right? So here's a list of terms I wished I'd known before birth for you to research further:

- antenatal
- Apgar score
- Braxton hicks
- forceps
- gestational diabetes
- incontinence
- induction
- meconium
- posterior
- prolapse
- showing (mucus plug)
- TENS machine
- vacuum cap (or ventouse delivery)
- waters broken.

But don't stop there! Keep researching as widely as possible, and investigating further on any term unfamiliar to you, or any definition that just doesn't seem quite right.

Acknowledgements

I have so much gratitude for the entire Bravemumma-hood. Your backing, love and support made this dream a reality – a published book. Thank you!

The list of individual people to thank could be longer than the actual book itself. So let's start with the people who have helped take this project from just another one of Steph's crazy 'big' ideas – to an actual book!

Tom – that one little word changed our world and lives forever. Thank you for saying 'yes' to Bali. We now know that 'having your wife back' is the best ROI and one that no amount of money could ever buy.

Andrew Griffiths – thank you, my sensei. For years I have admired your skill and mastery, and most of all you! The way you truly care for people is inspiring and heartwarming. You are an amazing mentor and anyone would be lucky to be able to work with you.

Michael Hanrahan – I feel so very lucky to have been introduced to you and the team at Publish Central. Thank you for your genuine support and encouragement. You knew exactly what to say and when it needed to be said. My fav is, 'Yep, just keep going, Steph, you're on the right track.'

Charlotte Duff – the editor everyone needs to have. Thank you for treating the words in this story with the dignity and respect they deserve. It was an absolute pleasure working with you. I look forward to teaming up for the next one.

Dave Stokes – thank you for helping me keep my promise to my bestie that this book will be available for everyone, especially those who are no longer able to physically hold a book. It has been an absolute pleasure working with you on this audiobook. Thanks for making it fun!

To these early supporters who were the very first to be brave and pre-order a copy. Thank you to Anita Struthers, Rebecca Kokineli, and April Alexander and Stacey Williams (who were at the exact same time).

Thank you to all the people who have helped me along the journey to becoming a mumma and beyond;

Tom (yes, again!) – your unwavering support is the very definition of unconditional love. You always have my back (even when I'm wrong). I love how you 'roll with the punches', even during the times when we feel we're wrestling the entire world. Your smile is the best thing ever. It was the one thing that kept me going in that delivery room. I know you were literally dying on the inside with fear about what was happening, and yet, you only gave me the best of you. You alone got me through. I am and will be eternally grateful to you for that. You are a wonderful daddy, husband and my friend. I love you, my Tom.

To baby Louis, my son – you are the most adorable little 'mini-me'. We are so blessed to have you in this world. I love you with every part of me. You make my heart sing.

To my parents Lyn and Steve – thank you for raising me to think that I could work hard to achieve anything in this world. Thank you for all the hard work you have both put in your entire lives, only to make our life better. Mum, thank you for birthing me, and thank you for making me a strong, independent woman who never gives up (much to your dismay at times).

To my sissy – thank you for being my sounding board (for all of those OMG moments) and being right there when I needed you, especially on this book writing journey. I'm so grateful that I have finally been able to find the words to tell you how hard things have been. I feel our relationship is only stronger now – and that's awesome.

Acknowledgements

My entire family are beautiful, loving, supportive people, who all achieve great things. You all inspire me to be who I am today. Thank you for your love and care. I love you all.

My mumma (grandmother) – your name is the inspiration for Bravemumma. I know you are looking down on me, smitten that you are now famous in a book. You always knew I would end up being a writer. Over all those years, and all those stories you wrote and sent to me, it just took me a while to catch on.

Jojo – I know how much you wouldn't be expecting this, but you are amazing! Our family has been so lucky to have met you. Your love and care for our little people is more than we could have ever hoped for. We knew from the moment we met you, you were THE one. You were the only carer who asked what Elsie liked (and she was only a tiny baby). You are our village. Throughout this writing journey you have taught me so much, and I admire your non-judgmental ways and thoughts about childbirth and motherhood. Thank you for always being there for me too. I love you as a true friend.

To our mates Si and Neety – we are blessed to have met you cool cats. Thank you for always putting your hand up to help out and making us feel like nothing is a problem – that's true friendship right there.

Dr Ali Bear Jones – our story is one of friendship that lasts the ages of time. As a young nineteen year old, you were my role model. I have always looked up to you and have been in awe of your courage and strength. Thank you for teaching me that you need to make a life, to have a life.

Sharn – my bestie. This all began with the notebook and pen you gave me way back in 2007. You told me to write down some things while on my cancer journey. I did. I just never shared it with anyone, except you. We have shared a thousand lifetimes' worth of experiences together, had more tea than all of China and loved more than the best-selling rom-com. This book's title was chosen by you. The day I came to tell you about the book, it wasn't a good talking day – but your eyes said it all. They lit up the world (as did your smile).

I knew by the look in your eyes that this was the right fit. I'm so grateful to have shared our endless numbered days together with you. I miss you and love you – every day.

And thank you to the special people I have met along this journey.

Simon Winder – because of you, I was able to be brave enough to feel I could welcome our little Louis into our world. Thank you literally holding me (and Tom) for those nine months. There is no way I could have worked through that level of fear without you. This birth experience gave me insight to what I'd always pictured childbirth to be.

Prof Dietz – when I first spoke with you on the phone years ago, I was astonished by how much I could relate to what you were saying. You were truly the first person I trusted who knew what they were talking about in relation to childbirth trauma. You were the person I wanted to envelop me and tell me it was all going to be okay. Your passion and dedication to this area is impressive. Women like me are very lucky to have people like you – working hard to help fix (or more so prevent) broken vaginas.

Elizabeth Skinner – thank you for your years of passion, experience and research in this childbirth space. Had it not been for your interviews with those 40 brave women (and their partners), along with your published works about harrowing birth trauma experiences, we would not have such an amazingly supportive organisation as ABTA.

Karlie Picton, my exercise physiologist – it's only been a short time since we started working together. And while we know my pelvic floor can never be the same, it has never deterred you from trying a million different things anyway. Thank you for your level of commitment to me. You're a real gem!

Kimmy O – as my very first lady boss I always admired your calmness and supportive leadership. Now after many years of friendship, you've shown me what true loyalty is. Thank you for being such a beautiful person and always supporting me. 'I take a look at the driver next to me – he's just the same.'

Amy Dawes – my fellow mumma. What you have achieved in your own trauma journey is phenomenal. Thank you for taking my hour-long call many years ago and supporting me at a really shitty time. Thank you for helping me understand that, no, what I was going through was not 'normal' and pointing me in the direction of professional help.

And finally ...

For my Elsie – writing this book and sharing it with the world demands a level of vulnerability and courage that doesn't always come easily to me. I worry that you will one day read these words and somehow feel responsible for the trauma I experienced during your birth. But I know that if I say nothing, nothing will change. And I'm called to do everything that I can to stop anything like this from happening to you, my Elsie. So, I wrote this book for you.

Tea for Two
A friendship steeped in love

Back in 2007, you gave me a notepad and scribbled a message in the front cover, expressing your love for me and your encouragement to write a book about my cancer journey. There is a book much bigger than that, however – one about you! Your inspiration and strength mean a thousand books should be written about you. This one is just the start. Sharn, this is for you, my friend.

www.ingramcontent.com/pod-product-compliance
Lightning Source LLC
Chambersburg PA
CBHW071457080526
44587CB00014B/2136